Our 'Journey':
One Couple's Guide to U.S. Surrogacy

RICHARD WESTOBY

ISBN: 978-1494456641

DEDICATION

This book is dedicated to my husband Steven and our amazing children Alexander and Liliana. Steven and I owe an immense amount of thanks to Angela and everyone else that was involved in our surrogacy journey – so this is also dedicated to you.

CONTENTS

1 Foreword

Steven and I first met on 27th August, 2005, in Mykonos, Greece. It sounds very cliché but I remember it as if it were yesterday. Our friend Stan, who had been trying to get us to meet for the best part of a year, finally succeeded in his mission. It was 11pm in a crowded, hot square and I knew that I had met the love of my life.

We had our first date on October 14th (as we both lived in London our social lives were incredibly busy, hence the 6 week wait), and have been pretty much together ever since.

In all honesty I never thought that I would get married as it was just not something that was ever on the agenda. But from the moment we met I knew that I wanted to share the rest of my life with Steven. In my mind I wanted the world to know that I had met, and wanted to marry, the most amazing man. So, after having been together for about 2 years, we started discussing formalising our relationship in the UK with a civil partnership.

Amongst our friends we were some of the first to go down the civil partnership route, and when we mentioned it there were some that were excited, some that were completely indifferent and some that said "Why would you do that?"

It is funny and interesting as I look back now, as we would experience exactly the same reaction when we started talking to the same people about the prospect of having children about 2 years later.

On May 24th 2008 we had our civil ceremony, attended by all of our respective family members and a handful of our closest friends. To most people perhaps that seemed to be the culmination of our romance and the start of the happily ever after. But in early 2009 we started to talk about the idea of us having a family.

I can't really remember what the catalyst to shift gears in life from living the ideal gay life to creating a family was, but it definitely seemed like the natural evolution of our relationship. By this stage we had been together for a number of years, and we started to try to figure out what the meaning of everything in our lives was.

We had bought a beautiful flat in London, we had a nice car, we travelled abroad regularly, staying in amazing hotels. I can definitely put this all down to the power of the 'pink pound', which is what you get when a gay man works and earns without having the responsibilities that go hand-in-hand with having a family. We basically thought nothing of our ability to do things that most couples would not think of doing as they start to save for their children's education or buying a house, etc.

Objectively looking, Steven and I spent the first few years of our marriage having the most amazing time. We genuinely experienced life in an exciting and thoughtful way. However it wasn't only about sharing our amazing lives together, and we began to think that would we like to share this with others. We are both deeply caring and affectionate people – why shouldn't we share this love with children – children of our own?

Deep down we knew that we would make great parents. Both of us had well-paid jobs, and that meant we had the financial means to make sure that a child would be financially well looked after. But we realised that wasn't the whole picture; we also had the emotional means to be great parents. We would be able to ensure that our child would be completely surrounded by the love that we had to share – and that was something that we both wanted so much.

Hence the subject of children became a discussion that we had on a regular basis. We started talking about it not only between ourselves but also with friends, colleagues and to anyone that would listen to why we could possibly want to have progeny! We did this subtly, as we felt that it was a good idea to get people's true opinion on the subject without projecting what we wanted them to think.

This book is an account of what we did during the whole process and why we did what we did at each step of the way. It is not meant as the definitive guide to surrogacy, so please do not take it as such, yet at the same time it is structured in a way that each chapter is a step in the process, and at the end of each chapter there are questions that you should be asking yourself. Hopefully this will allow you to become more informed about the process.

Everything in this book is, to the best of my knowledge, correct at the time of first printing. Every journey to creating a family is different, so there will be a variation on a theme, but I believe that the process is very similar – if it isn't, then I apologise. Obviously situations and laws change, therefore it is imperative that you do as much research as you can on how your journey will differ from ours. I am not a lawyer, an agency, nor an IVF doctor, and as such this book is what happened to us and is my interpretation of what we found along the way, so please bear in mind that there will be some differences to your journey.

Also, you will have to make sure that everything you are doing is legal in any of the places that you either reside or are looking at, i.e. surrogacy is illegal in certain of the US states. After reading this book I would advise that you contact a professional in order to run through your thoughts so that you are comfortable with the process.

Specifically, I would say this relates to anything to do with the law (in the US or in the UK) or with the immigration process. But when you are having that conversation with your lawyer, use the information in this book as a basis for a much more informed conversation with the professionals. This is a much better starting place for everyone.

This book really is not meant to be a memoir of our life together, but unfortunately in order to bring home some of the points it kind of has to be, so apologies for what might seem at times rather narcissistic! And, as I've mentioned, neither is it meant to be the 'right' way to do things nor is it meant to be the 'only' way to do things. This book has been written for people who want to be able to glean unbiased information from a couple who have been through the surrogacy process. We learned a lot as we went along and we are very happy to impart most, if not all, of this information to you so that all in all the whole surrogacy process can become more transparent.

Otherwise you, as someone who is not completely aware of the process, would run the risk of being taken advantage of. Therefore the aim of this book is to get you to a starting place with a level of information that enables you to have informed conversations with professionals involved within the surrogacy industry.

This book is supposed to help you at each fork of the road to make the right decision for you with as much information as you can possibly have. After all, this is YOUR family, and you should be able to create it the way that works for you.

2 Our 'Journey'

The start of something that would turn our lives upside down, but in such a great way... Picture the scene, The Standard Hotel in Miami, just before New Year 2010, Steven and I sitting in the sun, enjoying the pool area with beautiful people frolicking in the pool, lying around drinking martinis and basically enjoying the great sunshine that Miami has to offer. A complete opposite to the discussion that we were still having about whether to finally go-ahead with the surrogacy process that we had been pondering for months.

Of course, we got side-tracked and had another drink, once again procrastinating about the decision to go ahead or not. Then our friends Michael and Darren turned up. But before I carry on, let me tell you about these two – they are both very successful in their own careers, one is a lawyer for one of the biggest law firms in the world and the other is a highly respected interior designer. We always have a blast with them as they are fun, fun, fun, but not only that, they also have been the inspiration for us along this whole journey as they have twins – two lovely little girls.

We have known couples who have had babies but, really, we know Michael and Darren the best. They have told us all along exactly how it is, what the pitfalls are (and they encountered many) and what a joy it is to be a dad.

Anyways, back to the story; they turned up with their two girls and we all had lunch together. What a joy it was to be sharing calamari, bread, pasta, salad and everything that was on the table with two inquisitive little people sitting with us trying it all, spitting some out but generally loving life.... We didn't need to procrastinate any longer; we were going to go ahead with our surrogacy journey.

This book came about as, although we had friends who had been through the process, none of them had written it down in any great detail in order for us to be able to start making informed decisions about what we needed to do and when. After our children were born I was asked regularly by others for more information on how we did what we did and, after putting pen to paper, this book was born!

Having children, or making the decision as a gay couple that we wanted to have children, remains a mystery to me. One day I was perfectly happy living my life with my partner, and then the next we were thinking that our lives were not complete and that we needed to do something about it. I cannot pinpoint any single catalyst to why we decided to do it, just that we felt it was the right time for us.

3 Starting a Family

So we had made the biggest decision about whether we were going to go ahead or not. But on top of the decision to start a family, we needed to figure out how to go about it. Did we want to adopt, co-parent or go down the surrogacy route?

Co-Parenting is where you share the parenting role with another person with whom you are not necessarily in a relationship. We ruled out co-parenting almost immediately as it didn't feel like the right option for us.

We definitely went through the thought process of whether or not we should adopt but in reality the choice for us when we were deciding whether to adopt or to go down the surrogacy route was rather simple. In a nutshell we wanted to go down the surrogacy route as we really wanted a genetic tie to our children. After all, we had friends who had started their family through surrogacy, so we knew it could be done, and when we looked into adoption it firmed up our thought process.

We really believe that there are many children that are in need of a loving and stable environment, and so adoption would be the 'right thing to do' for society at large. We've been asked along the way why we didn't adopt, and it's interesting to wonder how many straight couples who get pregnant, either by IVF or naturally, get asked the same thing. I doubt many do, so why is there such societal pressure on a gay person who wants children to go down the adoption route?

I'm sure that is a talking point that could go on for days but when we did look at adoption, in our case, due to the average of our ages (for the nosey, it would have been 42), we were advised that we would be given a child of at least 3 years old. That is not what we really wanted, which would have been a new-born infant. At that age in a child's life it is very hard to think of what it could have been through to get to the stage that it needs adopting: abuse, neglect, or was it an orphan? One never really knows and, rightly or wrongly, that frightened us (admittedly probably not as much as what the child could be going through) but, still, it cemented our view that we wanted to go down the surrogacy route. So our decision to look at surrogacy was now made.

Before we go any further on what we did, it should be noted that there are two different types of surrogacy – traditional and gestational surrogacy. Traditional Surrogacy is a process whereby the woman who carries the baby actually is the woman that has also provided the egg that is fertilised. For us this opened up a whole host of potential issues as the surrogate would be genetically linked to the child, and therefore this needs to be thought through very carefully.

In Gestational Surrogacy the woman who carries the baby is literally just the oven, or in our case we called her the Tummy Mummy. We provided the sperm, we had an egg donor provide the eggs and then, once fertilised, they were placed into the Tummy Mummy for 'cooking'. But more about her later!

Intended parents, or IPs, are just that – the people who intend at some stage in the future to become parents. It's funny to be grouped into a classification like that because I've never really thought of myself that way but, anyway, it is a term that I will be using a lot throughout this book.

Currently (2013) everything surrounding surrogacy in the UK remains such a minefield. Without doing a lot of reading and talking to people (including lawyers) it is very hard to figure out what the law says. Everyone has an opinion on which parts are legal or illegal, who has the rights, etc..

As things stand, the one thing that I do know is that no third party is allowed to make money from surrogacy, hence why surrogacy agencies are illegal. Surrogates are not allowed to advertise that they actually want to carry a child for someone else, and neither are intended parents allowed to advertise that they are looking for someone to help them have a child. This situation is irrespective of sexuality.

Then, to further complicate matters, in the UK, birth-mothers have the right to change their mind about giving up a child from the day of birth up to 6 weeks later. This applies to mothers who have given up their children for adoption as well as mothers who are carrying children for other people (i.e. surrogates).

We heard of a straight couple who had a gestational surrogate carry their baby (the intended parents' sperm and egg), and after the birth of the child the birth-mother decided that she wanted to keep the child... They then ended up having to pay child support to the surrogate as, under UK law, she won the court case that ensued. We thought long and hard about this and really decided that if this happened to us we would be so upset at having to go through all the anxiety surrounding pregnancy and then not actually having the child. It would just create massive pain and anguish.

Next we asked ourselves in which jurisdiction we should do the actual process. We thought about looking at the various countries in which surrogacy is allowed, including India, Thailand, the Ukraine and South Africa, and of course we looked at the different cost implications of these countries.

Although one of the cheaper options, thankfully we didn't choose to go down the Indian route as they have now banned same-sex couples from having children through surrogacy. We also looked at the other countries. We have no physical ties to South Africa which is a prerequisite there so that option was ruled out, and then in all honesty the other countries just didn't appeal to us. So we went back to our original option, which was surrogacy in the US.

Why did we do this? For three specific reasons: 1) As Steven is American this gave us a tie to Steven's home country, and also 2) the

US has the legal framework tried and tested so it is all in place, and 3) surrogacy is understood and is now a more mainstream and, although complicated, is an understood concept.

Questions to ask at this point

a) Do you want to adopt, co-parent or go down the surrogate route?
b) If surrogacy is for you – in which jurisdiction will you proceed?
c) Can you be a traditional surrogate (if you're female) or will you need a gestational surrogate?

4 The Surrogacy Agency

So how did we then get to the decision-making stage about which agency to use? It is very much possible to do the surrogacy process yourself, but we thought that, just as we would not think about building a house without using an architect/general contractor to help us, why would we try to build a family without an agency that specialises in doing exactly that – building families.

Obviously there is a cost implication involved in using a third party to help with the process, but at this stage we had no idea exactly how much this was going to be. Unfortunately no amount of online research will actually tell you the final cost because it is such a dynamic situation where you can have a rough guide but not a definite number until it is all done! The number seemed to range from $100,000 to $125,000, but I will go into much more detail about the costs involved in Chapter 27.

Knowing now how the process works, it is interesting to understand that there are multiple options available when choosing a surrogacy agency – some agencies are one-stop-shops for the process, whilst others are not! Some will literally hold your hand the whole way and make sure that you do not have to think or worry about anything, and then there are others that will do the bare minimum. There are surrogate finders, and there are also people who say they run a huge agency and then you find out they were a surrogate mum who went through the process, thought they could do it and decided to just open up an agency as something to do.

In early 2010 we spoke with a friend of a friend who had just had a baby boy through surrogacy, and he recommended that we start researching online about the larger agencies in the US. It is amazing how just by typing in on the Internet 'surrogacy agency US' the two top agencies appear – they both must spend a fortune on PR and their Search Engine Optimisation, or they're just searched a lot!

In my experience the larger agencies have the ability to have a lot of staff on their payroll, but that does not necessarily mean they are good. A good question to ask an agency when talking about their staff is what their average staff turnover is – a large turnover means that the case coordinators who look after you during your process might not be there throughout your journey.

Once you have determined the size of the agency you can start to see how this will affect you down the line. For example, I have found that the smaller agencies typically have lower overheads and can therefore charge significantly less than the larger agencies. This to me is counter-intuitive as the larger agencies typically have in-house everything and should be able to benefit from economies of scale.

So, do you get better service from the smaller agency? It could be that their staff deal with multiple cases, so could they 'drop the ball' because they are too busy? Or, do they actually have the experience that you need for your specific case? By talking to the agency and doing research you should be able to figure out how the agency actually works, and then you can start to refine your selection down.

On top of looking at the size of the agency, it is worth finding out how the agency treats their clients – some separate out their clients by what they deem 'international' and 'domestic' clients – with domestic being clients that are US-based intended parents and international those clients that are intended parents from anywhere else in the world.

Why do they do this? I think that it is down to health insurance and whether or not the surrogate needs to have her own healthcare insurance or not. Also, anything around Americans doing surrogacy in the US is much easier, and therefore they can get their process started a lot quicker. Insurance is a minefield that I will go into in much more detail later in Chapter 7.

This naturally leads on to the question of how many intended parents the agency currently has on their books waiting to be matched, and what is the average matching time?

One of the very important things to think about as well is what happens if you decide that you don't like the agency that you are working with and you want to get any money back. The answer to this depends on many things, but if the company is attorney-owned (the American word for a lawyer) then there is a possibility that you could get money back, as attorneys are regulated under the legal bar rules, whereas agencies are not. Lawyers are allowed to charge for work that is done and earned but must refund anything that is not yet earned.

However, you will find that most attorney-run agencies will split their business into two parts: a) the attorneys (who do the contracts and court work) and then b) the 'agency' for everything else. Bear in mind that part b actually includes some legal stuff as well. For example, only certain states allow surrogacy and the agency needs to understand and explain to you which states allow it and which don't. But the main function of the agency part is the case management of your 'journey'. This is how some agencies are able to have part b unregulated and therefore they can turn this into a non-refundable part of their business.

This also has ramifications down the line as an intended parent should have attorney/client protection whereas they don't have legal protection from an agency. Attorneys (and anyone working for them) must act in the best interest of the client – all the time – and so long as the client wants to do something legal then the attorney should facilitate that. Does the agency have to abide by the same rules – no!

Therefore you should definitely ask how your agency will act if there is a conflict between the intended parent and the gestational carrier. In my opinion the attorney's client is the intended parent, and therefore you should always be their first priority and they should work to resolve any issues with your interest at heart.

Once you have refined your selection you should ask the agency a number of questions around the egg donors and surrogates.

First of all, ask how they find their surrogates. Is it by word of mouth and referrals from previous surrogates or is it online? In my opinion you would ideally find an agency where the majority of their surrogates come from referrals. I personally think that the word-of-mouth route is the best route because that means that someone who has been through the process with the agency liked how they worked and recommended them to someone else. I don't think that you would want an agency to find their surrogates from an online chat forum – just my opinion obviously! The reality is that if they medically screen well then it doesn't matter how they were found, but I think that it is worth knowing.

Other things to ask the agency include how many surrogacy births do they have every year and how many pregnant surrogates are on their books at the moment. Obviously supply is far outstripped by demand, but these are good things to know to get an all-round picture of the agency at that snapshot in time as well as how long your potential wait to find a surrogate will be.

Then another question to ask is whether or not the surrogacy agency actually do home visits on the surrogate to see how they live and the environment in which they will be carrying your child. This should be part of the background check that they perform (which also includes financial and emotional checks, etc.).

The final question to find out is what happens if you match with a surrogate and for whatever reason either party has to pull out. Typically there will be non-refundable fees on your side but what if the surrogate pulls out – how quickly will you be matched with another surrogate, what incremental fees do you have to pay? All very important to know up front.

Then, with regards to egg donor pools, most agencies will have an egg donor pool that they will recommend you use. If they do, then ask if their egg donors are medically screened before they are admitted to the egg donor pool. The reason behind this is because you could end up with an egg donor who on paper looks amazing but medically is not as good as one would think. Two alternatives that I touch on later in this book are to use your IVF clinic's egg donors or to use an egg donor facilitator.

You should also look to see what international exposure the agency that you are talking to has had in the past. This is a question that is very important because the agency should have some basic knowledge of how the process should work with regards to your home country – they won't be able to advise you legally, but they should have learned from their past clients and also they should be able to refer you to local professionals. Obviously parts of this book will help clients in the UK understand much more about the process but, as you are about to pay a lot of money to their business, you should see how they understand the ramifications in your home country of surrogacy.

On top of the international exposure you should also start searching online to see what kind of reputation the agency has. There are now many different websites that you can go through to find first-hand examples and information on what agencies have done and how they have treated their surrogates in the past. This is invaluable information for you to have and to take on board.

It is very easy to be blinded by a sales pitch, but listen to others who have been through the process. The reality is that there is nothing as powerful as first-hand information on why someone used an agency and what their thoughts were after having been through the whole process. On top of this I would also talk to as many people as you can, either online or personally, to really find out if the reputation matches the reality.

Since we finished our journey we have now come across a not-for-profit website that has a summary on most of the surrogacy agencies and IVF clinics. I wish it had been available when we were doing all our research http://www.menhavingbabies.org/surrogacy-directory/ I would look very carefully through this website and use this as part of your box ticking exercise on reputation!

Finally you need to ask the agency for a figure on what they think the whole process will cost you. Obviously, for most of us, cost is a major factor when making the decisions on which agency to use. I say this because there is a massive layer of opaqueness surrounding exactly how much the process will cost, and it is almost like deciding on a surrogacy agency because you like the staff and trust what they say. Most will give a ball-park figure on what it costs, but we found that the final amount went far over what they said it would!

As I mentioned, the numbers range widely. We were quoted a total around the $120,000 mark. I go into much more detail about costs in Chapter 27, but included in the figure you receive should be information on:

- How much the surrogate will receive
- How much the egg donor will receive
- How much will be the legal fees you have to pay for both surrogate and egg donor
- How much the case management fees will be (for the agency to manage your process)
- How much the IVF clinic should be charging (this may be a rough estimate and is not part of their remit but it is good to have this included in the rough total figure)
- How much the health insurance is going to cost you.

To be honest, the amount of decision making to get to this point was exhausting – so many different things had to be looked at, researched and debated that eventually you just grind down and sometimes you just go with an easy option. Not necessarily the most effective way of making life-changing decisions, but in our case that was how it happened.

It is also amazing how many more agencies have appeared in the time that has passed since we started the process, and how much more information on the agencies themselves is now online. However, there does not seem to be any one place to obtain a step-by-step guide on how to do surrogacy... Hence this book!

Questions to ask at this point

a) Do you want to use an agency or not?

b) What kind of agency are you looking to use, i.e. a big company vs. small company?

c) Is the agency attorney run and, if so, how is the business split? How much money will be returned if you decide to use another agency

d) How will the agency resolve any conflicts?

e) What is the total number of staff and their turnover rate?

f) Are you being treated as an international or a domestic client? What are the timing implications of each?

g) How many intended parents does the agency have waiting to be matched and how long is the average wait?

h) How does the agency find most of their surrogates? What background checks are done (home visits, financial, emotional)?

i) How many surrogacy journeys does the agency do yearly?

j) What happens if the match breaks down?

k) Where do you want your eggs to come from – surrogacy agency egg donor pool vs. IVF clinic egg donor pool vs. other routes?

l) Has the agency that you are looking at helped a lot of international clients or do they focus primarily on the US?

m) Find out what the ball park costs are and find out where and why these costs could increase.

n) What is the agency's reputation with intended parents and surrogates?

5 Surrogacy Agency Chosen

At this stage I'm making it all seem straightforward and simple. The reality is that it isn't quite like this. We found that we did research online, filled out some questionnaires to ask for information and then all of a sudden we would have a constant barrage of phone calls, emails and Skype messaging all asking whether or not you've made your decision yet.

Looking back on it, I realise that we had already self-selected to use the agency closest to Steven's parents, but the reality is that for any agency this is a business – and a very profitable one – so the agency will go after every client that asks for information very aggressively. Bear that in mind.

So, once you have chosen the agency that you feel works for you, you start negotiating the 'agency contract' with the surrogacy agency. This delineates exactly what they will and will not do. For us this process took about 6 months, as we were unhappy with some of the provisions and we asked them to be removed.

For example, we decided that we did not want photos of our children to be allowed on any marketing material that the agency used. We also had to negotiate with the agency on specific contractual items, such as the costs involved if we go through the surrogacy process again using the same surrogate, for which they would get a fee irrespective of whether we used the agency or not!

This was our individual process and every process will be different. Our only piece of advice is to really go through the contract very carefully and make sure you understand exactly what you are getting into with the agency – because once you sign up, there are potentially a lot of non-refundable fees! So check anything that is non-refundable, and make sure you fully understand exactly what it means and the implications for you.

The main thing that we looked out for was what would happen if either we or the surrogate pulled out at any stage for any reason other than one driven by a doctor's decision. For us, if we pulled out then all of the non-refundable fees were due; if the surrogate pulled out then the agency would find us another one for no extra cost.

An obvious option for you at this juncture is to retain another lawyer to review the surrogacy agency contract and to point you in the direction of specific things that they think need discussing. This lawyer should detail out for you all of the fees that you are paying, explain the potential outcomes if things go wrong and, of course, point out anything that is non-refundable! The reality is that most of the contracts are pretty straightforward and standard, but there are definitely some things that are negotiable (see above for what we negotiated).

When we signed up with the agency they asked for the first stage of payment to be made. This covered a vast array of things and was around one-third of the total expenses that they said we should be willing to pay. This amount covered:

- The first instalment of the agency fee
- An egg-donor fee
- Office expenses
- Drafting and negotiating surrogate and egg donor contracts
- Paying the legal fees for both the surrogate and egg donor
- All of the psychological exams that both the surrogate and the egg donor would go through
- An advance on the travel and other expenses for the surrogate
- A trust administration fee.

The trust administration fee is charged because basically all the money that the agency think you will have to spend on the process is sent up front to the agency. It is then put into an escrow account (or a trust account) and used as and when required, i.e. when bills have to be paid or payments to certain people have to be made. I will give some more thoughts on this in Chapter 8, but this is a major thing to think about. Is the trust covered if the agency goes bankrupt? Is the money segregated into an account that is legally yours, or does the money belong to the agency as soon as you send it through to them?

I don't remember specifically being psychologically screened by a professional. That said, we definitely had an informal conversation with the surrogacy agency about why we wanted children, as well as discussing in what kind of environment they would be brought up. The people that we spoke to at the agency are trained psychologists with children of their own, but were we evaluated? Who knows – the one thing that they could do was very much talk us through some of the questions that we had with regards to the actual process, as well as the thought process that they went through.

Up to this point in all of your dealings with the surrogacy agency you will be given a certain level of information on how they operate. Obviously they don't want you to take the information and then go through the process on your own, so they keep it very simple and very brief. But once you transfer the cash into the escrow account the agency knows that you are serious and the process really kicks in.

You are asked to write a document that includes details about your childhood, your education, your life and also why you want to have children. You should also be asked to write a letter for the surrogate to read when the agency shows her your profile. We were very honest in this letter about what we were looking for in a surrogate, why we felt that we were at the right stage in our lives to have children and, most of all, about how much we appreciated our surrogate for even thinking of having children for us. You are also asked to send through some photos of you and your family so that the surrogate is able to put names and faces together.

You will receive multiple emails containing lots of information on how the agency physically runs the process, as well as emails starting to show you surrogate profiles and egg donor banks and providing information on anything else they can give you with regards to health insurance, but the most important thing is that this payment also puts you onto their waiting list.

The agency will try to manage expectations by saying that it is typical for the wait time to be anywhere between 3 and 12 months just to find the surrogate! Our agency has numerous lists of clients, so you can never really know if you are first in line or tenth, but this is in a way understandable, and I will explain why later on.

Questions to ask at this point

a) Check which fees are refundable and which are non-refundable in case you don't use the agency to do a specific part of the process, e.g. finding the egg donor.

b) Have you thought about what you would put into your profile that will be shown to the surrogate?

c) What is the escrow trust account structure (see Chapter 8)

6 The Surrogate

We signed up with the surrogacy agency in the middle of June and in 4 weeks we were contacted by the agency asking if we would like to have a Skype conversation with a potential surrogate… HOLY MOLY, how did that happen so fast, after all the discussion detailing how long it was going to be! Of course, it brings everything home that the process is really starting, which is incredibly scary and yet exciting at the same time!

We said that we'd love to, so they sent her our profile and they sent us through three different pieces on Angela, our potential surrogate.

First of all was the **psychosocial evaluation** of Angela. This evaluation (which you pay for) contained information on her background, her relationship history, her pregnancy history, her current family situation and her commitment to the surrogacy process, as well as her expectations from you and, finally, the psychosocial worker's opinion on whether she would be a good surrogate.

Secondly they also sent us through the **questionnaire** that Angela had filled in detailing much more information about her. There are about 200 questions ranging from her birthday to menstrual cycles to drinking habits, and then the complicated ones about why she chose to be a surrogate, what she is expecting from the process, how many embryos she would like to carry, what to do about abortion if needed … basically a very thorough piece directly from her on her.

And finally there was the **gestational surrogate reference checks**, which is a piece written by a friend (who will act as a support person) on Angela.

So, there we were in July 2011 trying to figure out the time difference between London and Arizona (a state that doesn't change their clocks ever), and we had our first Skype call conversation with Angela. Right from that moment we knew that she was an incredible and very special woman and that it was going to happen. Thankfully, Angela also felt the same way. We both got in touch with the agency after the Skype saying that we had an amazing feeling about her and that we wanted Angela to become our surrogate or, as I've mentioned before, our Tummy Mummy (endearing or annoying, I will leave that up to you to decide).

As Angela was a first-time surrogate we didn't have the opportunity to ask her what she liked or didn't like about her previous surrogacy experience. I think that is a very important part of the framework to ask any experienced surrogate so that you can all start to set your expectations of how your relationship is going to work. If she didn't like something last time, then you don't do it this time – if she loved something, then you do that!

At this stage of the process we really were wondering if we should interview more potential surrogates and what other information we should be asking Angela as, after all, we had just made a rather large life decision based on a 30-minute Skype call. The answer to that was we didn't interview anyone else because we went with our gut feel that she was doing this for all of the right reasons. It might seem odd, but we really felt a bond with her just from that initial call.

One thing that we didn't really think of at the time, but that was pointed out by the agency, was that under UK law any birth mother (in our case the surrogate) is always considered the legal mother and has all the rights as such. This isn't so much of a huge problem, as it can be extinguished by going through a legal process once you return, but a problem arises if the surrogate is married. I say this because if she is married, then her husband is recognised as the father and not the intended father, who is in fact the sperm donor.

This can seriously complicate matters, especially with immigration! Therefore this is yet another major thing to take into consideration. One way for a married surrogate to not have her husband put onto the birth certificate is if he denies any knowledge of the surrogacy process being undertaken, which to me is a very complicated way of going about the process.

I lightly touch on this because you really should start to think about things like this and raise questions with the surrogacy agency on how they manage the process on their side. Later on in this book I will walk you through the process of birth certificates, court processes and everything that we undertook and the reasoning behind every decision.

So, it could be that, like us, you sign up with the agency and a surrogate comes along that is single, widowed or divorced, and the agency thinks, "We don't regularly get these, therefore we will give this woman to the next person on the UK waiting list". In this way you can leapfrog others who have been waiting for a while.

At this point you should find out from the agency or the questionnaire if your potential surrogate has had her own child before. Most IVF clinics will not take a surrogate who has not been pregnant before. On top of this, her last pregnancy needs to have been without complications, as this is something that the IVF clinic will want to know. Why would they do this? If a surrogate has a history of going into early labour or of having to have bed rest for weeks on end, then this is something that you, as the intended parent, should find out, as this will drive your decision to proceed or not.

In our case, Angela had two boys – one was 14 and the other was 8. She is originally from the Philippines and had moved to the US just before her 18 birthday. Since that day she had worked extremely hard to make a life for herself. We loved the fact that she had worked three jobs to put herself through university and had even done a Masters whilst working and pregnant. She told us a story of how her final exam was the day that her eldest son was due to be born and she kept asking him not to come until she was done with the exam. Lo and behold, shortly after putting her pen down she went into labour! Now that blew us away. Whether it was her unborn child listening or her body responding, who knows, but what amazing timing!

At the time of the process she was 34 and single and, although we never really asked the underlying reason why she was doing the surrogacy process, we really feel that it was to be able to help her children go to good schools. That is the kind of selfless person Angela is. To this day we keep in touch with her and regularly send photographs and emails on how the children are doing. And this brings me to another point – you should have in mind what kind of relationship you want with your surrogate. Do you want them in your life forever or just through the pregnancy?

One of the most important things that you must start thinking about at this juncture is whether or not your surrogate has her own health insurance. I will go into health insurance in the next chapter, as it is such a large and very important topic to cover that it really needs a full chapter dedicated solely to it.

Having now been through the process, we realise that actually it is a good idea to look at which states allow surrogacy and which don't. Your agency should cover this for you, and they should know where it is allowed etc., but it is always good practise to double check. It is something we didn't think about at the time but that is worthwhile at this moment in your journey. You do not want the baby born and only then finding out that in the state the child was born you have no legal rights to actually take that child home.

There is a great link that one of the surrogacy agencies, Creative Family Connections, updates regularly. As US law is ever-changing, their website shows different states and where surrogacy is legal and where there are certain challenges that could come about. The links is http://www.creativefamilyconnections.com/state-map-surrogacy-law-practices This will help you to look at the different states that the agency is proposing your surrogate comes from and should help to narrow down your thoughts. From this website you can see that Arizona, where Angela lives, is open to surrogacy, although there are certain hoops that need to be gone through, more so than a state like California for example.

One final thing to also take into account with regards both the surrogate and the egg donor is that if they are of Native American Indian descent then there are legal complications surrounding the child. This is because under US law the tribes from which either the surrogate or the egg donor descends have a right to take the child once it is born – therefore unfortunately you must avoid using surrogates from these communities.

Now that the decision had been made to go with Angela, and before the legal contract with her was negotiated, the second payment became due to the agency. The amount that we had to then pay through was the remaining two-thirds of the total that they told us we would need to transfer over to them. This amount of money that went into the trust account included:

- The second instalment for the agency fee
- The legal proceedings fee (for post birth)
- Payments to the surrogate (transfer of embryo, clothing allowance, monthly fee)
- Carriers payments
- Insurance payments
- Egg donor payments
- Extra contingencies for expenses.

Also, at this stage, as I've just mentioned, the legal process with the surrogate kicked in. The agency acts as your lawyer and will 'guard' your interests, but they can also act for the surrogate. So is that a potential conflict of interest? Very possibly… So it is always a good idea to find out exactly who you are paying (as you pay for all of the negotiations etc.), and to see where there is either a conflict of interest or whether the agency is getting any fees from the outsourced lawyer. In our case, they farmed out the work to a specific lawyer that acted for our surrogate (at least that is what we were told) and we then negotiated the terms of her contract with this lawyer.

Some of the things that we negotiated included:

- The fact that our surrogate agreed to assist in us being named on the birth certificate post-birth
- What to do in the case of abnormalities with the child
- The surrogate agreeing to undergo medical testing
- The surrogate agreeing to be celibate for the period around her IVF treatment
- How many IVF cycles we would go through in case of a failed cycle
- How many embryos to implant at each cycle
- What would happen if there were to be a miscarriage.

This is to name just a few of the things. HOWEVER, in my mind, the most important of these is what to do if you decide not to continue with the pregnancy.

Selective Reduction (a nice way of describing abortion of an embryo, or the term used for when you decide not to continue with one of the embryos) is a major topic currently in the US. There is a couple who had not had this conversation with their surrogate and ultimately they decided they wanted to abort due to genetic abnormalities. The surrogate decided that she wanted to keep the child and, as you can imagine, this has caused major problems as to custody, payments to the surrogate, medical bills, etc.

The other thing that the contract will detail is a list of all of the costs that are involved if the surrogate has to undertake specific procedures (amniocentesis etc.).

In our experience, we definitely felt that the law firm both on our side, and the one that we had retained to represent Angela, actually charged a huge amount of money for a standard contract that they probably roll out to every parent. We also felt that the surrogate's lawyer always amends specific clauses that your agency will tell you just to agree to. Once again it is probably standard procedure for them to do this, but unfortunately there is nothing that can be done as you need a water-tight legal contract, especially in the US. For example, we negotiated with Angela's lawyer how many days she would receive off if she undertook a C-section, and how much money she would receive per day.

Before you sign the actual contract with the surrogate you should arrange for your surrogate to be medically screened by either an IVF clinic or a gynaecologist. This is to make sure that she is still able to medically carry a child, as the last thing that you really want is to negotiate the contract and get completely emotionally involved with the surrogate only to find out that for one reason or another she is unable to carry a child.

In our case Angela had not been medically screened by an IVF clinic, so we decided to fly her from Arizona to Connecticut and to meet up with her at the same time. In this way we could actually meet her, as well as allowing her to go through all of the medical testing.

To note that the medical testing itself actually has to be done at a specific time of the month for the surrogate. This is around the second or third day of her period cycle and entails a medical test, a blood test and an overall health check. Thankfully Angela passed on all fronts and, although she suffered from a very minor raised blood pressure, the IVF clinic thought she was a perfect candidate. She was given a tablet with a very low dosage of medication to maintain her blood pressure, and we were assured it would have no impact at all on her ability to carry, nor on the children's wellbeing.

Questions to ask at this point

a) Is your surrogate married or single?
b) Is surrogacy legal in the state in which your surrogate lives?
c) Is your surrogate of Native American descent?
d) Has she carried her own children before and was the last pregnancy without any complications?

e) What kind of relationship do you want with your surrogate?

f) If your surrogate has been a surrogate before what did she like in the past journey and what kind of relationship does she want with you?

g) Does the state in which your surrogate lives allow pre-birth orders for out-of-state residents, or is it a post-birth state?

h) Have you discussed selective reduction as a couple and with your surrogate?

i) Is your surrogate willing to be medically screened before signing any contract? This will enable you to see medically if she is able to carry a child.

7 US Health Insurance

One of the most important parts of the whole surrogacy journey in the US is health insurance. As I mentioned above, it is very important to understand the actual situation that you are in with regards to healthcare, because it could mean the difference between you spending $10,000 and $100,000 more than you had budgeted.

In the US, everything to do with healthcare costs a fortune and, as such, having insurance cover is a must. However, it is not as simple as that. To most non-US intended parents, the insurance system in the United States is a complete mystery. It is important that one understands that US insurance is primarily private insurance that is governed by contracts written by the insurance companies. These contracts have been upheld in the US courts when insurance companies fight a case against a claimant so long as their language is clear and unambiguous.

As a result, if an insurance company chooses to exclude coverage for something, they may do so, as long as they are clear about it. In other instances, insurance companies who have failed to clearly exclude surrogacy still attempt to avoid coverage by using other exclusions to claim that they are in fact not bound to cover a surrogate's maternity expenses. Hence there is the argument for a need for insurance policies that expressly cover surrogacy to be in place.

With regards to US health insurance, there are terms used such as 'in-network' or 'out-of-network' that need a little bit of explaining. Basically what in-network means is that your insurance provider in the US actually has a range of contracts with different doctors, specialists and hospitals, each of which has agreed a predetermined rate for the services provided. This rate includes a portion that you pay (also called your co-pay) and a portion that the insurance company will pay.

So, when you are looking at any doctors to do anything you need to make sure that they fall within the network of providers that have agreed rates with your insurance company – or 'in-network providers'. If not, you will have a doctor that is 'out-of-network', and typically this will cost you more as there are no pre-agreed rates, as well as higher co-pays etc. Our obstetrician, Patricia, was in fact out-of-network for the babies but in-network for maternity care, and we decided to go ahead with her even though we knew it would cost us more because of how we felt about using her to do all of the medical provision for the babies.

It should be noted that in the event of an emergency most insurance policies will cover a portion of the emergency care no matter where you are, even if it is within an out-of-network provider. Once the condition is stable with regards to either the surrogate or the babies, then they will generally be moved to an in-network provider to continue their care.

So, now that you have the basics of US health insurance it is important to break down into component parts the different types of insurance that you will need to buy.

Complications Insurance

When doing the retrieval of the eggs from the egg donor and then implanting of the embryos into the surrogate there are two sets of insurance you need to cover anything that could potentially go wrong at this stage of the game.

The first insurance that you will take out is for the egg donor and the second is for the surrogate, and it is called complications insurance. In a nutshell, this is an insurance policy that covers both women in case anything goes wrong with the procedure. The reality of both of these two insurance policies is that they are relatively inexpensive at approximately $150 each and our policies provided cover to both surrogate and egg donor of $250,000.

Surrogate Health Insurance

It is important that the surrogate has health insurance to cover her from the time of implantation right throughout the pregnancy and up to the birth of the baby/babies.

Under the new healthcare reforms that are coming into place in 2014 my understanding is that all policies will cover maternity costs. The reason for this is that maternity will be classified as a right for women or 'basic coverage', which means that in and of its own right maternity cannot be excluded by insurance companies.

Therefore, assuming that her policy does not specifically exclude surrogacy, in theory all of the surrogate's maternity costs should be covered. It will also mean that the premium for the health insurance policy will be based on the age and the zip code of the person applying.

For me this remains a grey area. How will the insurance company find out that the birth is a surrogate birth, as they are not allowed to ask all mothers-to-be if they are carrying a surrogate baby? The only way that I can think they will find out is if they ask to review the charts post-birth and see the notes associated with the birth. Once again, that is assuming that the healthcare practitioner notes that it was a surrogacy on the charts.

When we went through the process we wanted to find a surrogate who had her own health insurance for two reasons. The first reason was that our surrogate would have continual coverage. This means that her policy is in existence already and therefore there would be no waiting period for the maternity benefits to start. Secondly it meant that we would have one less thing to worry about from both a bureaucratic and practical perspective.

However, we realised that if the surrogate we were shown didn't have her own policy, then we would have paid for a policy to cover her maternity expenses. This will be the case from 2014 if the surrogate's policy specifically excludes surrogacy.

If your surrogate has insurance coverage then most agencies will charge you a fee to read through the policy terms and conditions to make sure that she is eligible to be covered throughout the surrogacy process. However, even if the agency reads through the policy and says that there are no exclusions, you can still be liable if the insurance company try to claw back any fees paid.

So if you are being charged a fee keep this in mind, and if possible negotiate that fee down or negotiate that this fee covers the surrogacy agency fighting against the insurance company on your behalf (they are lawyers after all!) especially if they dispute any payments.

That said, I think it is important for you to understand what the policy contains in order that you are once again making an informed decision! Bearing in mind that I am neither an insurance broker nor an insurance lawyer, my understanding of insurance for the surrogate is in the decision tree below. This is very simplified, but it should help you to start to understand the logic behind this whole process and enable you to talk about it to an insurance broker or your surrogacy agency.

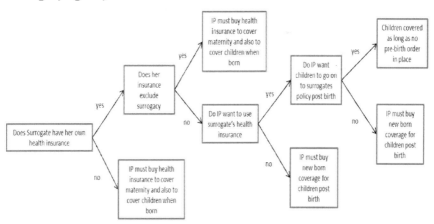

If you need to buy a policy for your surrogate then historically the insurance broker community recommended that intended parents look at a Lloyds of London policy specifically tailored for surrogacy.

The Lloyds of London policy could be used as a primary insurance policy (to cover all of the maternity and birth costs) or, if you are able to find insurance elsewhere, it could be used as a 'back-up' insurance policy.

As a back-up policy it will only start if the surrogate's insurance claims are denied by her primary policy would leave you without coverage. This is an expensive option as the premium is paid up-front, costs a lot of money and is only 80% refundable if no claim is made.

My understanding is that under the new healthcare reforms there will be many changes to policies and different options available. Predominantly this will be due to the fact that maternity is now a basic coverage right although there seems to be massive confusion around when a women is able to apply for insurance as well as the different ways that she can apply.

Therefore I recommend that you discuss this whole point at length with your agency and/or with an insurance broker so that they can give you all of the options available at the time of starting this journey.

Surrogate Life Insurance

At the same time as buying the above surrogate health insurance, the agency that we were dealing with got us to purchase a life insurance policy for Angela. This policy would pay out $100,000 us in the event of her death before the children were born, and it would pay out $250,000 to her family or beneficiaries.

The $100,000 figure comes about as it would roughly match all of the expenses that we would have incurred up to the point of her death. For us the premium of $287 was not a huge amount of money, but it is worthwhile to have – also I think that the actual premium would be dependent on the surrogate's age, general health and her zip-code.

New-Born Coverage (Post-Partum Coverage)

Finally, most babies will need some form of hospital treatment immediately after they are born, especially if they are twins, which are classified in the high-risk category. This is the part that can be incredibly expensive if you do not have coverage for them. It is called New-Born Coverage.

It used to be that all American women who chose to be a surrogate would have their own health insurance and could put the intended parents' new-born onto their policy. Now, however, most insurance policies explicitly exclude surrogacy from their maternity coverage, so if the surrogate adds the baby to her policy and puts all of the hospital's birth charges through the policy then it could flag up to the insurance company that this was a surrogacy arrangement.

Quite how the insurance company is able to find this out I'm not sure, but apparently they can. The insurance company then has the ability to retroactively deny any claims that the surrogate has put in to be covered throughout her pregnancy and claw back any payments that have been made.

If surrogacy has not specifically been excluded, and you are able to use the surrogate's health insurance for maternity, then the likelihood is that you are able to carry that coverage over to provide cover for the new-born child.

BUT if you are going to be using her insurance to cover the children then you are not able to have a pre-birth order, as that will stipulate that the children are yours from birth and therefore the surrogate is unable put them on her policy. You will have to go down the post-birth order route which is a topic I detail more in Chapter 21.

New-born coverage is also the part where non-Americans seem to have a problem, as it is very difficult to get US coverage for the child of a non-American parent.

Lloyds of London have a policy that is very expensive but, as I've mentioned above, there are policies such as Allianz that might cover a singleton. It is worth thinking creatively about this policy as, in other instances, such as where one of the intended parents works for a global company with US offices, or where one of the intended parents is an American living abroad, it could be that the intended parents can obtain insurance that will cover their dependents from birth and thus save a lot of money.

We thought that it could be that Steven's work insurance would have coverage for his dependents born anywhere in the world, but unfortunately it excluded the US. So back to the drawing board and we had to look for an alternative.

Thankfully in our case, as Steven is an American expatriate, we approached HTH Insurance and took on their policy. This covered Steven, his spouse (they recognise marriages and civil partnerships from other countries) and both of our dependents, so both of our children.

This will potentially all change under the Obama-Care act that will be coming into force in 2014, so it is really well worth quizzing any agency that you are talking to about the insurance part of the puzzle and what solutions they are proposing.

Apologies for the amount of information that I'm trying to get across to you. I realize that not only is it a lot to take on board but also that it is quite complicated! But, to summarise, what you will need to look at and buy are policies for:

The surrogate

- Complications insurance in case she has any form of medical complication from the IVF procedure
- Health/maternity coverage to make sure that she has health insurance coverage from the time she contracts with the couple to the time that she is released from the hospital after the birth of the baby
- Life insurance coverage in case she dies at any stage during the process.

The egg donor

- The only coverage required for the egg donor is complications insurance in case she has any complications from the IVF process.

The baby/babies

- Immediately following the birth most babies require some form of hospital treatment and this needs to be covered by post-partum or new-born coverage

Below is the above explained as a time flow diagram:

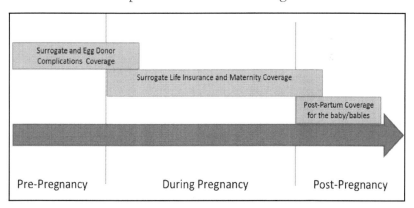

Once the children are born you would be forgiven for thinking that everything is done and dusted, but alas it isn't. Two months after our children were born we asked the surrogate if she had received any invoices from the hospital with regards to the babies. She had, and they had been forwarded on to the surrogacy agency and we believed that everything was being taken care of.

Then, 9 months after the babies were born, we received an email from our surrogate stating that the hospital was chasing payment of $15,000 for one of the twins. As you can imagine this was a large surprise for us. It turns out that due to a mix-up, one of the bills had not been submitted to the insurance company and had been sitting in a financial controller's unpaid accounts for months.

Therefore, it is well worth checking with your agency to find out what is going on with regards to insurance co-pays or claims put in by the hospital to the insurance company or any bills forwarded to the agency. I would also confirm with the agency a few weeks after the birth that they have called the hospital to make sure it has submitted all of the invoices through to the right insurance companies, and that everything is being processed properly.

I have had multiple debates with people about this stage of the process. We typically discuss whether or not it is ethical to have a surrogate put the new-born on to her policy and have her insurance company pay the hospital bills when you know that you will be taking the child once it has left hospital?

Whether it is right or wrong whenever I am having this discussion I say that it is not for me to decide. Once again I believe that it is all about getting every option on the table and then letting the intended parents make their own informed decisions.

Questions to ask at this point

a) Does your surrogate have her own health insurance and does it exclude surrogacy?

b) Does your agency allow you to use your surrogate's health insurance?

c) If you are going to use the surrogate's health insurance for your new-borns, you cannot have a pre-birth order. Is that ok with you?

d) Do you have your own health insurance that will cover your dependents from the minute they are born?

e) Are the doctors that you are thinking of using within the health insurance network of approved doctors or out-of-network?

f) Once the child is born, has the agency been in touch with the hospital to make sure that the correct amount has been billed to the correct insurance policy?

8 Trust/Escrow Account

I briefly mentioned the trust/escrow account before. For us, this was run by an internal team at the surrogacy agency that we used therefore I can only talk about how it worked for us. You might find that smaller agencies will outsource this to a professional company, and therefore you must do your own due diligence on the outsourced company for the reasons I mentioned before.

If you are using a surrogacy agency at this stage of the process you should start receiving monthly accounting from the trust accountants. You will see that, immediately, all of the non-refundable fees are removed (typically all the fees that are agency-related charges are non-refundable). It is worth going through the trust account statements with a fine tooth comb, as things crop up that either need explaining or that are just wrong.

For instance, our agency used an outside company that books travel for the surrogate and the egg donor. Bear in mind that you pay for all of the travel required for both women and one person to accompany each to get to the IVF clinic for the testing as well as the transfer.

Because our surrogate and egg donor lived so far away and they had to get overnight flights to the IVF clinic, we thought that it would be nice for us to arrange a car to collect them from JFK airport and drive them to the clinic. Most people use a mini-van shuttle that entails lots of stops whilst other people are dropped off at hotels, but we thought that, seeing as these two women were giving us huge gifts, the least we could do was pay for a car service to collect them from the airport and take them straight to their hotel. Realistically, the shuttle is a lot cheaper, but what a hassle, especially after overnight flights!

When our egg donor flew in, the car that we had asked to be arranged wasn't waiting for her. Every time an egg donor or a surrogate travels they should be given an out-of-hours or emergency number to contact, so the egg donor called the emergency number and spoke to someone at the travel company. This person told them to just get into the first available taxi and take that to the hotel where they were staying. That would have been fine if the ride was 15–20 minutes but the reality is that it was nearly 2 hours!!

The bill for this was then sent to the agency, who just added it to our account. So, instead of the $140 car service that I had agreed to pay it was a $411 taxi ride… Now, unless I had gone through the account with a fine tooth comb and questioned exactly what that was, we would have paid it, but I refused to pay for something that they messed up, and the agency paid for the difference.

On top of the agency payments that you have in the escrow account you also have to budget for the IVF programme itself. So, when you're doing your calculations you have to add this on to anything that the agency tells you, unless they include it in their total calculations.

Questions to ask at this point

a) Does the agency you are using have its own escrow/trust account?
b) Are you willing to go through the escrow account every time you receive it? if not, find someone that will do it for you
c) What are the financial safeguards in place for the escrow/trust account?

9 The IVF Clinic

At some stage in 2010, I had been watching the television and a CNN program about two gay men in Manhattan having a baby came on. It went through their whole journey as well as it could in 45 minutes, which was quite interesting. During this TV show an IVF doctor was featured – Dr Michael Doyle. He came across incredibly well during the show, and so I stored that in the back of my mind for when it came to the decision of which IVF clinic to use.

We once again went online and researched different clinics across the US from California to Boston, and we sent a number of emails requesting to talk to the IVF doctors in the clinics. We found that the services offered are very similar, but the methodology of providing those services differs greatly.

For example, some doctors charge for an initial Skype consultation on how they run their practice. This can range from $400–600 depending upon with whom you are talking. Others don't – they assume that the initial consultation should be part of the whole service. Dr Doyle is one of the latter and so, after dealing with two doctors on the West Coast, we set up a Skype call with Dr Doyle.

We actually ended up spending about 3 hours of his time on different occasions talking about all the permutations of what could happen, what could go right, wrong, etc. He patiently walked us through all of the steps that he could and introduced us to his team of people in order to talk genetics, as well as to get access to his egg donor pool. And yes, we decided to use his clinic for our IVF process.

Aside from the fact that he is incredibly personable and knowledgeable, we also decided to use an IVF clinic on the East Coast of the US as there are numerous flights from the UK to New York and Boston, both of which are close to his clinic. This would allow us quick travel time to fly over for the testing, as well as only a 5-hour time difference. These are very important things to keep in mind when you are choosing anyone and everyone during this process – where are they in the US, how quick can you get there and the time zone difference for conversations or issues.

In the interests of transparency, as someone who has been through the whole surrogacy process I now act as a business development person for Dr Doyle in the UK. This works incredibly well for us both, as I get to detail my journey to other prospective parents and Dr Doyle has the added value of gaining first-hand stories that I can supply; that's how great an impact the people at CT Fertility had on us, as this is something that I would not being doing if I didn't feel that this was a great clinic with great people.

Once again, http://www.menhavingbabies.org/surrogacy-directory/ has a list of most of the larger IVF clinics and their ratings from parents who have been through the process. It's something that I would love to have seen when we were doing our research, although I suspect we would have still chosen the same IVF clinic!

On the Skype calls that we had, one of the things that we spoke about with Dr Doyle was how they have a bank of egg donors and why these could be different to a surrogacy agency's bank of egg donors. The reason for this is that the IVF clinic actually pre-screens all of the egg donors before they are allowed into the egg donor pool in order to make sure that they are medically able to donate. I've mentioned this before – make sure you know if your egg donor has been medically screened and approved.

However, the most important thing is the success rate for fertilisation and transfer through to pregnancy – we were happy with the numbers that we heard, and of course with the fact that we wanted to try for twins and that Dr Doyle was happy with us doing this, etc. He said that we had approximately an 85% chance of getting pregnant if we implanted two embryos, and on top of that we had a 50% chance of it being twins.

To me that was a great probability. However, I then asked how many cycles a year they do because, of course, if it is a low number then in reality it isn't that good. He said that they do between 250 and 300 cycles a year! That is a lot of pregnancies!

We also asked a question that he'd never been asked before, which was how could his clinic guarantee that the right embryo would be implanted in the surrogate. This was a genuine concern of ours, because can you imagine if you end up with someone else's baby at the end of the whole process? Needless to say, Dr Doyle laughed and said that the procedures in place would never allow that to happen, and in his 20-plus years he'd never seen anything like that happen.

Finally, to labour a point, you need to really think about the cost angle again. This is something that the surrogacy agency may or may not include in the total number that they quote as this is realistically out of their sphere of influence.

With our clinic there was a variety of options that we could choose from, ranging from one to four cycles – it is probably best to check with the IVF clinic what they do and how they price each individual programme that they offer.

We (unfortunately) know too many couples who have been through multiple cycles and have been unsuccessful every time, and therefore we decided to opt for a programme that would allow us to do four cycles.

This programme gave us the most amount of comfort as by the fourth cycle, Dr Doyle has a 99% pregnancy rate! Obviously with anything to do with IVF there is absolutely no guarantee that you will get pregnant and opting for this programme cost us more than a single cycle, on a per-cycle basis it worked out as the best option for us.

On top of this decision, in the US you are able to choose to do further genetic screening. For example, we both did a test where we spat saliva into a little test tube, and that was then sent off to a genetic testing company in order to see what diseases we were both genetic carriers of. We then asked the egg donor to do the same and compared the results.

Obviously if the egg donor and either Steven or myself were carriers of the same genetic abnormality (i.e. we had specific alleles that were coded to carry a disease), then we would have chosen someone else as our egg donor because the probability of transmitting this through to the child would have increased.

An example of how recessive and dominant genes are passed down by alleles from two parents to the child is below[1] and, as you can see, if either of us and the egg donor were carriers for cystic fibrosis (CF in the diagram), we would have had a 25% chance of having a child that suffers from cystic fibrosis and a 50% chance of the child being a carrier. Ultimately there would only be a 25% chance of the child not being affected, which is something that neither Steven nor I wanted.

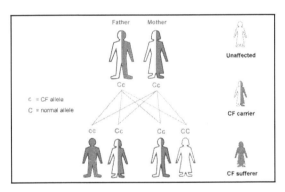

At the same time as doing the spit-test, another option for the intended parent is to undertake a PGD test. PGD stands for Pre-Implantation Genetic Diagnosis, which is where some cells are taken from the embryo and tested for disorders at a chromosomal level.

1

http://www.bbc.co.uk/schools/gcsebitesize/science/edexcel_pre_2011/genes/genesrev2.shtml

This testing is done before the actual implantation of the embryo and it allows intended parents to implant chromosomally normal embryos which should increase the chance of survival as you are removing one limiting factor by only using genetically viable embryos.

You typically have the choice of which day you would like to do the PGD testing, days 3 or 5. At day 3 cells are taken from the embryo itself and biopsied whereas at day 5 the cells are taken from the part that will become the placenta and then biopsied.

There are pros and cons to both days and multiple risks to the embryos. At day 3, there are fewer cells to choose from and more cells on day 5. We asked if taking cells at day 3 meant the embryo would end up missing a leg or an arm. Apparently not, the cells at this stage of development can turn into anything so taking a few isn't a problem… phew.

A day 3 PGD test means that you have the time to implant a 'normal' embryo on the optimal day 5 whereas if you do a PGD test on day 5 then if the testing can't be done quick enough then you have a day 6 implantation (less optimal) as the testing can take up to 24 hours.

Finally, for me the most important thing was that PGD testing on day 5 is actually less invasive to the actual embryo as no cells are being removed from the embryo sac, but from the placenta cells.

In the UK there are legal implications of PGD testing whereas in the US, to the best of my knowledge, there are not. And on top of this, PGD is an expensive procedure to undertake.

This is also the time where one is able to select the gender of the embryo to be implanted. We decided that we didn't really care if we had a boy or a girl because it was such a gift to be able to actually even get to the stage of implantation that we wanted to let some things be up to 'Mother Nature'. So we did not gender select on our embryos and we didn't undertake any PGD testing because we'd already done the spit-test. That had come back with no matches, so we felt that PGD was one step that was unnecessary for us.

Taking into account the above decisions and optional extras you should ask the IVF clinic exactly what the 'normal' programme includes. For us it included:

- Psychosocial evaluation of the egg donor
- Medical and genetic screening of the egg donor
- Counselling and treatment of the egg donor
- Egg donor case management and her fee
- Donor medications
- Surrogate medical fees
- Father medical fees (1 or 2 sperm sources)
- IVF and laboratory procedures.

So now it seemed that we had all of the building blocks in place to get the process started. The agency, surrogate and IVF clinic had all been chosen and we'd negotiated legal contracts with all of them. But hold on, we actually need to find the eggs!!!

Questions to ask at this point

a) How far is the IVF clinic from an international airport?
b) How does the IVF clinic rank with regards to statistics (i.e. pregnancy rates), and also what is their reputation amongst surrogates, egg donors and other intended parents?
c) How much time are they willing to spend with you going through questions you might have about their IVF programmes?
d) How much are their IVF programs?
e) Do they pre-screen all of their egg donors?
f) Do you want to undertake genetic testing to see what genetic disorders you are a carrier of?
g) Do you want to do PGD on the embryos?
h) If available, do you want to gender select?

10 Choosing An Egg Donor

Choosing the eggs should be a simple thing to do, but in reality, once again, it took forever to do. One thing to note at this time is that there are two types of donors that you are able to choose from – an 'anonymous' donor or a 'known' donor.

Anonymous is exactly what it says – you are able to choose from a profile that will have all of the donor's information on it but it will be redacted to such a point that you are unable to ever get in touch with her. A 'known' donor is someone that you are actually able to talk to and get to know a little bit so that you can understand first-hand her motivation behind becoming an egg donor.

We had decided very early on that we didn't want to use eggs donated by any friends for our baby. We did have a couple of our friends volunteer to donate their eggs to us, which was such an amazing thing for them to offer, but we felt that we wanted someone that we didn't know to give us the eggs.

This way we would be always able to make all of the decisions around the children without having someone else involved. We know some couples who have taken a sibling's eggs and then fertilised with the other partner – this way there is a real genetic link to both families in the child, and that is an amazing thing to be able to do but it just wasn't what we wanted. Also, both Steven and I actually have only got brothers so this wasn't an option!

We had also decided that, even though we didn't want to use friend's eggs, we did in fact want to use a 'known' donor. We wanted this because, aside from the multiple physical features that one is able to choose from, you can aim to understand what makes that person who they are and, hopefully, how those qualities (along with yours) will translate in your children. You can talk about what the egg donor's aspirations are in life and get a feel for what makes them tick.

Another piece of logic behind our decision to have a known donor was that if our children one day want to know who their biological mother is, and why she did what she did, then at least we would have that option. One hears many stories of adopted children spending their lives on a quest to find out who their birth mother was and why she did what she did, and we just felt that knowing our donor was a way for us to avoid all of the potential heartache that a quest could entail; we know and understand that one day it could be that our children ask to get in touch with her, and as things stand we have that ability.

Also, we thought that it would be prudent from a medical perspective; if we need to be able to get in touch with the egg donor for any medical or genetic reason then we know how to do this. And it also has to be noted that this is also a vice-versa situation; if our egg donor has children of her own one day and needs a genetic match for any reason then our children could possibly help.

So, back to where did we find the eggs? The surrogacy agency has an egg donor bank, the IVF clinic has an egg donor bank and then there are multiple other sites: eggdonor.com, conceptual options and fertility bridges to name a few. Of course we got in touch with them all and asked to see their donor's profiles.

We spent at least a few weeks asking to see more information on egg donors, and typically the ones we liked had just been 'reserved' or were already being used by another couple and were currently 'in cycle' (i.e. we would have to wait for another 3–4 months until they had been through a cycle and were able to start the process again). Rather a frustrating process.

We did wonder about the stories that one hears about choosing super-models from California that are Olympic sportswomen with *Sports Illustrated* cover pages and a stratospheric IQ to match – that would be the ideal woman for an egg donor, but the reality is that, even if she did exist, we probably wouldn't be able to afford her eggs!

When we were going through the donor profiles it was a very surreal experience because you are looking online at the potential mother of your future child. The different egg donor pools are all structured in a different way, but in general you will receive a lot of medical information, educational history and a few photos. We filtered the criteria down according to what we wanted, but some of the filters that we could have used included things like race, religion, height, weight and educational level attained.

In the profiles one gets to see not only a lot of details about the donor but also medical details about her siblings, parents and grand-parents. I felt like I knew more about the egg donor and her biology than I did about Steven's family… very strange. We actually decided that we didn't want anyone who had a family history of any form of genetic cancer (i.e. breast cancer), and we did want someone that was educated up to university level. Apart from that we were very open to suggestions.

We decided to go through the profiles in rounds. In the first round we both went through all of the lists individually and moved names and profile numbers into a separate list so that we could then go through these and discuss them. We then compared our respective shortlists, and if there was a match then that person went on to round 2. In round 2 we went through in much more detail with regards to their family history, and then we discussed which donors we liked and why.

The ones that we agreed on went to round 3. By round 3 we had narrowed our profiles down to five donors. Time for more judging of a person by looking at their profile on paper – really awful to have to do, but we had to come up with a donor somehow. That got us down to two donors, and then finally figured out the one we wanted as our first choice and the other as a back-up. The one we liked came from our surrogacy agency and the back-up came from an external egg donor agency.

Asking to talk to back-up led us to discover something that we didn't realise before. When we signed up with our surrogacy agency we didn't notice that, irrespective of which egg donor we chose, we would be charged a non-refundable egg-finders fee by the agency. So this meant that if we used the back-up, we could potentially end up paying a finder's fee twice. Once to our surrogacy agency and another fee to the people who found the actual donor that we used.

We ended up discussing this at length with our agency. The agency said that they have agreements with a number of other entities where they could share the finder's fee. If we found an egg from someone they didn't have an agreement with they would try to get one in place, but the fee would still be higher than if we used the agency's egg bank because they would take the external fee, split it in two and use some of the money we had paid to the surrogacy agency to cover that half. The other agency's half would have to come from us.

Confused? We were… But in a nutshell – we had already transferred $6,000 to our surrogacy agency, which for ease I am going to call Agency A, and we were looking at the egg donor bank of an external agency, which I'm going to call Agency B. If Agency B found us an egg donor they would also charge us a $6,000 finder's fee, but Agency A would pay half of the fee across from the money we had already paid them, which means that we would have to pay an extra $3,000 on top of the original fee. So that would equate to a total of $9,000 instead of the $6,000 quoted originally … UGH!

Luckily, during the discussions on using an external egg donor agency we were told by our surrogacy agency that the egg donor that we wanted as number one was in fact available, and we were asked whether or not we would like to reserve her. We said yes immediately and asked to have a Skype call with her.

The surrogacy agency set this up for us and we chatted. Obviously it was really awkward for all of us, as how do you start a conversation with "Why do you want to donate your eggs?" or "We're really nice people, so hi!" But we did it, we really liked her and she matched the profile that we had been sent through. On top of that, she reminded us both of Steven's nieces and her family seemed very close and very down to earth – two factors that really made us very comfortable with her as our choice. We had our egg donor. Her name is Jessica.

So, from that moment on we had the final piece for the foundation of our family. Obviously we still had to go through the legal process and, although some IVF clinics will tell you that you don't actually need to have a legal contract with the egg donor (they have one signed with her), I felt that for completeness of the whole legal process that we should have a contract with her.

Questions to ask at this point

a) Do you want to use a friend, family, a known or an anonymous donor?

b) Does your agency charge a non-refundable egg donor finder's fee, or are you able to choose the egg that feels the best choice for you?

c) Is your egg donor a proven donor – someone who has been through the IVF process before and has proven that she is able to produce a sufficient enough amount of eggs for the fertilisation process?

d) Is your egg donor a 'super' donor – someone who is proven and who has in fact produced over 20 eggs?

e) Has your egg donor been medically screened by the IVF clinic? (Which if she fulfilled the criteria in c) and d) above, she should have been and would have passed.)

f) Do you want a legal contract with your egg donor or does she have one in place already with, say for example, the IVF clinic?

11 Getting Pregnant

At this time there is a lot of introspection going on as individuals and as a couple. You are in effect choosing the other side of your child's genetics and the genetic mother of your future child. This is subconsciously what people do when they walk into a bar and meet that someone special for the first time, but we were actually doing it on the computer by choosing an egg donor. A very strange moment in our lives!

On top of this introspection there was also a lot of discussion in our household about the nature versus nurture argument that is always brought up around gay people. We really did a lot of thought about how it would be for our children growing up in the world with two dads. Would they be bullied at school? Would they also turn out to be gay? Would they be thought of as different? In fact this whole process was incredibly thought through at every step, as it is not like two men can just one morning wake up and have the conversation where one of them says, "Darling, guess what, I'm pregnant".

We both thought long and hard about what values we want our children to have, what kind of family we want to be and how we want to bring them up. However, time and time again we kept coming back to the fact that we just want our children to be happy and to have self-confidence and self-esteem. We want them to know that they are loved and were deeply wanted by us, so much so that we went through this whole process in order to have them. Frankly, as long as they have that, then as a family we can deal with all of the other things that life will throws at us.

At this stage in the bureaucracy process Angela had passed her medical screening, she had passed her psychological testing and we had signed all of the legal paperwork. Jessica had passed her medical screening and had signed all of the legal paperwork – so from a bureaucratic standpoint both women were ready to go – there was just one more thing for us to do.

When we signed up with the agency they said that before we would be able to do the transfer of the embryo to the surrogate we would have to have our Last Will and Testaments in place. This is actually a very important thing to consider because, if Steven and I were to die whilst the surrogate was pregnant, where would the child or children go?

We talked with three people in our lives and asked them if the unthinkable happened, would they look after our children? Thankfully they all said that they would, so we prepared our wills. We sent a copy of these to the agency, who then told the IVF clinic that we were now ready to proceed as all of the building blocks were in place for us to start our family.

The agency took control again and started the whole formality process with the IVF clinic. They will get in touch with the surrogate, the egg donor and the clinic to arrange times for the surrogate and the egg donor to undergo their medical screening with the IVF clinic (if they have not already done so), and for both women to start their IVF treatments at the same time in order to get their menstrual cycles in sync. It is very important that this happens, as even if the surrogate is 1 day off then the whole process will have been wasted – the eggs will be able to be fertilised but they won't make it to the implantation step.

I don't really understand how this can be monitored and it is therefore up for debate. If both the egg donor and surrogate are saying that they are taking their meds, how is it possible for anyone to really make sure they are? In my opinion, this is something that the IVF clinic should be doing – they should be monitoring who does what and when via blood tests for different hormone levels and also via ultrasound tests, which will enable them to check that the women are doing what they are supposed to be doing. It will also lead to the IVF clinic triggering the release of eggs at the best time.

Early in January of 2012 Steven and I flew to New York for a few days where, for FDA (US Food and Drug Administration) reasons, we had blood and sexually transmitted disease tests done. This has to be undertaken within a specific period of time before the fertilisation, so we thought that we'd do it on a Thursday and then spend the weekend in Manhattan before travelling up to Connecticut to start the physical process of making a baby!

The IVF clinic gives the intended parents and the egg donor a week where the retrieval could happen – this is because they don't really know how the egg donor is going to react to the drugs that stimulate ovulation. In our case it took right up to the Friday, so almost the whole week that we had allowed. Jessica had been in Connecticut for 5 days at this stage, and so we arranged with Jessica and her husband to sit down with them over supper and get to know them a little bit better.

Realistically this could have been very awkward, but in fact they were just wonderful. Steven and I were waiting in a restaurant in Bridgeport, Connecticut, with multiple scenarios running through our minds of how the evening was going to be, so when Jessica and her husband turned up we had already had a couple of drinks to steady our nerves!

We spoke at length about Jessica's family, as well as about the fact that she was studying for her Masters in child education, as she loves being around children. Her husband was incredibly supportive about her decision to be an egg donor, and I think it was good for him to meet us too, as obviously we were forever going to be linked to his wife (even if we don't have regular contact with her). He was a trainee lawyer working really hard to buy a house for them both to live in so they could then start a family. All in all they were absolutely lovely.

Needless to say the dinner went by in a flash, and before we knew it we were saying goodbye for the night and that we were not really sure if we'd see them the next day but that, if we didn't, then best of luck for the egg retrieval in the morning.

So, on Thursday at 9 a.m. we appeared at the IVF clinic and were directed to a waiting room. We had decided that we wanted to do a 'fresh transfer', which in essence meant that we would be using fresh sperm to fertilise the eggs instead of frozen sperm. The reason behind this was that Dr Doyle had explained to us that the success rate of fertilising eggs with fresh sperm was about 78% over 65% when using frozen sperm. Obviously we wanted to do everything to have the best rates as possible, hence fresh sperm.

I had always assumed that they would take a sample from me and a sample from Steven, mix them together and then let Darwin and his 'Survival of the Fittest' theory take its course. However, under FDA rules this is no longer allowed; we both had to produce individual samples and the clinician would use each sample to fertilise the eggs separately.

So, about 15 minutes later one of the technicians came and collected Steven first, gave him a plastic jar and led him off to another room. Then it was my turn. How awkward is this – you have to go and 'produce' a sample for them to be able to fertilise the egg, all of the pressure AND there are a number of people in the waiting room all knowing what you are doing – just so embarrassing. Then again, all the guys are in the waiting room for exactly the same reason and we're all pretending that we're just watching the TV on a random morning!

Anyway, I get to the room and there is a hospital bed, a TV and a rack of porn magazines. I thought it would be interesting to see what the magazines were like, and I opened up one of them. I nearly burst out laughing – a person who had been in before me had taken photographs of his partner and cut the photos up so that he could stick his partner's face over the pictures of the guys. Seriously, it was just what was needed to make a very sticky situation (excuse the pun) not so tense!

Once I was done, I left the room and there was a bell for me to push to let the technicians know that a sample was ready for collection. I collected Steven from the waiting room and off we went for breakfast… As you can imagine, the conversation was just surreal, "So love, how was that for you!"

Later that day we were told that Jessica's retrieval had gone well. She had produced 12 eggs, they were being split six for Steven and six for me and the fertilisation process was underway. All very surreal!

At this point we had asked which type of fertilisation they were doing – normal or ICSI. On TV one always sees a magnified screen of the egg and then a big needle coming in and injecting one sperm into the egg – this is called ICSI (intra-cytoplasmic sperm injection) or IMSI (intra-cytoplasmic morphologically-selected sperm injection). In our case, because the sperm on both sides were looking normal – i.e. they were 'swimming' as per normal expectations – they were letting nature take its course. I can only assume that meant they had the sperm and had just mixed it up with the eggs.

One thing to note is that specific medication can actually interfere with your ability to get pregnant. This is the case with the drug Propaecia that stops your hair from falling out – one of the contra-indications in their blurb in the packet is that there is a risk of the drug causing abnormalities of the external genitalia of a male foetus. This is because male semen can carry tiny amounts of the drug, which then gets to the foetus and could potentially affect its development. For this reason Steven was advised to stop taking it 3 months before the transfer.

That evening we received an email from the technician saying that the fertilisation had taken place and in the morning they would review where we were. So we waited with baited breath, and the following morning we received the news that all 12 eggs had fertilised naturally and were now sitting in their temporary home of an incubator.

There they sat for 3 days before the clinic sent us another message saying that, of the 12, one had not progressed but that 11 were still going, which meant that they would continue growing them in the petri dishes until day 5 after fertilisation. Apparently this is the optimal time to take the best embryos for transfer.

The day after the retrieval Jessica left to fly back home and Angela arrived – the two most important women in our lives at this moment unfortunately did not get to meet, which would have been an amazing experience for us. But such is life.

So, there we were, Angela, Steven and I in the hotel lobby in Connecticut with not a lot to do apart from talk about our respective lives, our thoughts, our values and everything to do with us becoming parents. Angela (as a mother of two boys) is well versed in the role of a parent and was fantastic throughout this time; after all we didn't really 'know' her and it could have just been a few awkward days, but it really wasn't.

She told us all about her life growing up in the Philippines until the age of 18, moving to the US and all of her struggles, and then she talked about her children and her dreams, and the more we got to know her the more we fell in love with her – she is just all around an amazing woman.

Unfortunately, because Jessica had taken longer to ovulate than we had originally hoped, our schedule meant that Steven had to leave the US in order to get back to his job on the Sunday night/Monday morning red-eye. I could stay until the embryos were 4 days old, but unfortunately that meant neither of us would be there for the transfer of the embryos to Angela.

As we had decided we wanted to have twins, we asked the IVF clinic to transfer the best two embryos to Angela. At the same time we asked the technician if he could photograph the embryos before they were transferred and he said that he could do this.

I find it astounding that we have actually got the below pictures of our children when they had been fertilised for only 5 days!

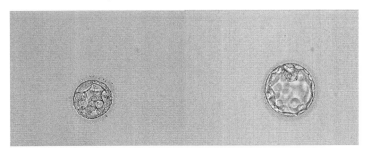

This was the period that we were dreading – up to this point pretty much everything that had been done was done in a medically enhanced environment, almost a protected platform, and every process and procedure had been undertaken with utmost care to produce the desired end result – a pregnancy. This next part was now down to God or nature or whatever you believe in. So the massive thoughts for us were: "What if they didn't take?"

As I mentioned above when discussing the costs and why we chose the most expensive package available from the IVF clinic, we know so many people who have been through the heartbreak of transfer after transfer with the embryos not taking.

We know exactly how hard this has been on the couples involved and on their relationships, and on top of that we also know exactly how much financial strain this has put on them, as it costs so much money to do transfers time and time again. And then, to top it off, as if the emotional and financial angles were not enough, after every failed attempt there is a 3-month waiting period before you can really start the process again, as both the surrogate and the egg donor have to go through a natural cycle.

So, on Thursday 12th Jan, 2012, we had fertilised the eggs and then on Monday the 16th January our 5-day-old blastocysts were transplanted into their Tummy Mummy.

Questions to ask at this point

a) What values do you want your children to have, what environment do you want them to grow up in and how do you think you will act as parents?

b) Who is monitoring both the egg donor and surrogate to see that they are responding to the IVF medications?

c) Can you do your sperm test locally or do you have to fly to the IVF clinic to do it? Locally obviously will save you a lot of money, but it needs to be in a manner that is FDA approved.

d) Do you want to be at the IVF clinic for the retrieval and implantation?

e) Do you want the IVF clinic to take a photograph of the embryos before they're implanted?

f) Do you have your Last Will and Testament in place?

g) Have you spoken with the people you would like your children to go to in case you die so that they are aware of your plans?

12 Early Pregnancy

We then had to just wait… 4 days of anxiety and trepidation and just wondering if the whole thing had been a massive disaster until Angela was able to have a blood test to see whether or not the transfer had up to that date been successful. Sharron from the IVF clinic called me up on the 20th January as I was having breakfast with a friend Lisa in Los Angeles. I remember exactly what she said: "Angela's HCG level is 199, which is a very early indication that you are pregnant! We will do another test in 7 days' time and that will confirm the new level and whether or not we think it is progressing normally." I burst into tears and Lisa just stared at me… she had no idea that we were either aiming to have babies or that we were on the verge of being a family! Of course we had a glass of champagne with our omelettes!

Another nervous wait ensued until the 27th January when Sharron called up again and said that the HCG levels had gone up to 472 and that they were very high, which, although it could have no bearing at all on anything, meant that she thought it could well be the twins that we desired. Another wait, and on the 31st January we received another call from Sharron saying that things were progressing rather nicely and that Angela's HCG level was now 2666!!!

Could it be that we were pregnant on the first IVF attempt and that we were actually going to have what we really wanted – a set of twins? But, of course, we would have another wait until the 6-week scan when Angela would have a vaginal ultrasound to confirm everything.

We debated whether or not we should fly to Arizona for the 6-week scan but, as much as we really wanted to be there, we just couldn't justify the cost. So, Angela went to the scan on her own and with the 9-hour time difference she called us afterwards which was late in our evening. The transfer had been successful and both of the little embryos had taken – we were expecting twins!! At this moment in time we felt that all of our hopes and dreams were coming true.

We decided early on that as Angela had had her transfer on a Thursday we would email her every other Thursday to find out how she was doing. We really didn't want to overwhelm her every day with our anxieties of what she was eating, when she was exercising or what she was doing every minute of every day. After all, she had already had two pregnancies of her own and knew what she was doing – you really have to put a huge amount of trust in your surrogate, and that is why it is so important to have her screened properly. Also, for us, it was very important to go with our gut feeling that she was going to put the babies first.

We decided that, as we had not been able to go to the first scan, we would fly over for the 10- and the 20-week scans. As we were spending a lot of money on the whole process it really makes you focus on where it is possible to save cash. Therefore one of our tasks was to figure out how to use up all of our air miles to get trips scheduled to coincide with the two scans.

For the 10-week scan we managed to get a direct flight on British Airways (who have one flight a day to Phoenix), and then for the 20-week scan we had to do a random round trip from London to Los Angeles to Phoenix to Chicago to London on Virgin Atlantic. But all the planning was worth it!

For the first trip to Phoenix for the 10-week scan we arranged for Angela and her two boys to join us at The Boulders Resort & Hotel in Northern Phoenix for the weekend. We wanted to spend the weekend with them all and to really get to know her and her boys much better. We met at the medical centre where she was going to have the scan and waited patiently for the doctor to arrive; whilst he did we had a lovely chat with Angela about how she was feeling, what she was feeling and how her weeks had been since we'd last seen her.

We finally got shown into the room and before we knew it we were looking at a scan of two peanuts with tiny little very quick beating hearts – as you can imagine, we both welled up with tears and Angela grabbed both of our hands and just squeezed. The man doing the scan asked if we wanted to take some photographs of the screen, and of course we jumped at the chance to do so.

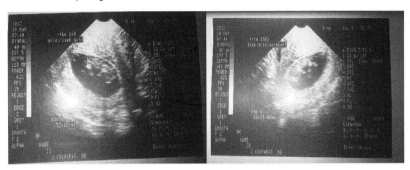

At this stage we were not able to really make out much from the images apart from the heart and a rough shape with a very big head! We decided at that point that we would like to know what sex the babies were as soon as we could. Frankly, it wasn't like this whole process was filled with enough surprises, and we wanted to be able to mentally prepare for the arrivals.

We maintained contact with Angela throughout the next few weeks by email and, obviously, now that we had spent more time with her we really felt that we were getting to know her more and more. We asked her how the pregnancy was progressing and if it was different to the times that she was pregnant with her own children. Obviously it was because this time she was carrying twins and not a singleton, which had a massive impact on her body. She was a lot more tired, retained a lot more water and was generally feeling very lethargic. But that didn't stop her getting up every morning at 4.30 a.m. to drive to her office, work 10 hours and then come home to look after her boys. Remarkable!!

Then it was time for us to fly again to Phoenix in time for the 20-week scan. It was a very different story. By this stage Angela had started to show her pregnancy a little bit, remarkably though not a lot. She said that she was talking to the babies every day and that she felt one of them continually on the move – the other one just stayed put. Bizarrely this was the case throughout the pregnancy – one kept on wiggling, the other didn't move! She also said that she felt like exercising a lot, so she was walking a lot more than normal and swimming too – all because she felt that she needed to be extra healthy for the babies as she wanted the best and most positive environment for them to be growing in. Once again we were so lucky to have found such a remarkable woman as our surrogate!

This time the scan was actually in the hospital where Angela had been going for her check-ups. We didn't really know what to expect as, this being a surrogacy, we were going to be two dads and Angela in the room with the ultrasound technician. We entered the room and the technician was very aloof and not very chatty... Not a good sign!

However, when the images started appearing and we grabbed Angela's hand the technician almost did a double take. She realised that this wasn't us using Angela as a vessel to carry our children, it was much, much more than that. The technician could see that we have such an amazing relationship with Angela and that we were obviously incredibly thankful that she was giving us this gift. Her attitude perceptibly changed and she started chatting away and taking a lot more snapshots of the different parts of the babies – and in general just being a lot nicer.

As Angela had said to us before, one of the babies was continually moving or, as the technician said, always trying to get into the picture! Eventually the technician asked us if we wanted to know what sexes we were having, to which in unison we replied: "Yes".

Angela turned to her and said, "I don't need you to tell me, I already know – I've done this before and I know what I was looking at when I was looking at it". The technician had Angela whisper in her ear, she nodded and then said to Angela, "Go on, you're right". Angela squeezed our hands and said, "You are having a boy and a girl".

Yes, tears again welled up and we just couldn't talk. How incredibly exciting; everything we had ever wished for was coming true, pregnant first cycle, twins AND a boy and a girl … just perfection. Once again we asked if we could take photographs with our phones, as you can see they had changed from being peanuts into little people!

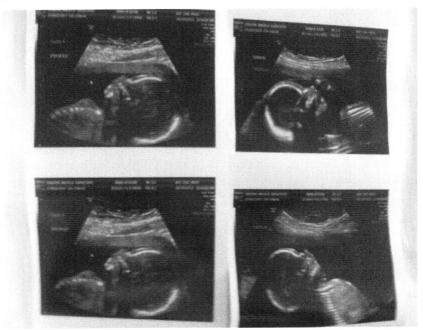

Questions to ask at this point

a) Can you justify travelling out for the scans at 6, 10 and 20 weeks?
b) Ask again what kind and quantity of contact do you want with your surrogate and does she agree to it?
c) Do you want to know what sex of baby you are having?

13 Maternity Nurse

About 6 weeks in to the pregnancy, Steven and I were talking with some friends of ours who had a maternity nurse help them through the first few weeks post-birth. In fact our friend who had given birth was adamant that she was going to do it all herself, but about 2 weeks in she was at her wits end and was speaking to her mother who said very calmly, "Don't worry, someone will be there in a few hours to help you out". Her mother had organised a maternity nurse months beforehand knowing full well that her daughter was going to need help. So we started looking in Arizona for someone who potentially would fit the bill.

Once again I was on the Internet trying to find information on baby-nurses (as they are called in the US), and in all honesty it was quite hard to find. Only later on did I get the reason why – apparently a lot of women in the US feel pressure to do it all themselves, and if they end up getting someone in to help they are viewed as a failure. I mean, how it is possible to think that way – we knew that we were going to need help, and a lot of it!

Anyway, I finally came across Desiree Nessline's details online and saw a newsreel clip where she had been called the baby-whisperer as she has an amazing knack with babies. I emailed, and we arranged to meet when we were in Phoenix for the 10-week scan. Of course I did a lot of email research on her, as well as reaching out to the references that she had sent me, so we felt that we knew her very well before we actually met.

So after the scan with Angela we got into our rental car and drove to meet Desiree at a Mexican restaurant. It was pretty much an instant liking – in fact, when I think about it, everyone that we met along this way we just felt was 100% right for us and the babies. Even though she spilt salsa all down herself, spoke at 100 miles an hour telling us about her life, how she looks after new-born babies, LOVES her job and can't get enough of helping new parents learn how to cope, we decided to hire her. And thankfully she was available around the dates we wanted her – she told us that she normally gets booked by her clients the minute they find out they are pregnant; that's how in demand she is.

We wanted someone to be with us 24 hours a day, 6 days a week for 6 weeks to train us on the actual day-to-day of being parents, as well as to start sleep-training the babies. Our logic behind this decision was that a) we didn't have a clue what to do with a baby and b) we wanted someone impartial to teach us. The other thing that we really loved about Desiree is that she is all about the babies having a routine.

We now understand fully why she was so adamant about the babies being on a routine – for us and our lives it is amazing. Frankly, the children love it as they know what is happening when, and to this day they sleep through the night off the back of her training! I will go into more details about her routine in Chapter 22 with a brief outline of timings in Appendix 3.

14 Obstetrician–Gynaecologist

In most situations, surrogates who have had children will have an obstetrician–gynaecologist (Ob–Gyn) that they have used before and who delivered their own children. This is also the same for the hospital in which they delivered their children. This is not something that the surrogacy agency will really get involved with, as they believe that the surrogate should know and trust fully the doctor with whom she wants to work, and that that is a choice that is fully up to her. This is something that is very important as the surrogate needs to feel comfortable with the doctor who will be monitoring her, as well as with the hospital in which the birth will take place.

So, go back a few weeks to the time that we did the transfer. We had been speaking to a great friend of Steven's who lives close to the IVF clinic and we had arranged to have lunch with her. At the lunch she brought a friend of hers who is an obstetrician in Connecticut. The reason behind this introduction was because he had actually been to medical school with a woman who was an obstetrician in Phoenix and he wanted to introduce us to Patricia. In fact, she had delivered his children!

We emailed with Patricia numerous times and had a couple of telephone calls but with the time difference it was very difficult to actually have a meaningful conversation. Therefore the weekend that we were at the Boulder Resort in Phoenix we also thought that it would be a great idea for us to arrange her.

We had spoken with Angela about the obstetrician that had delivered her two children, but she was no longer in touch with him. So after discussing it with Angela at length we all decided that on the basis of the personal recommendation we wanted to ask Patricia and her team of staff to look after Angela and the babies during her pregnancy.

Due to this we felt that it would be a great and very informal way for us all to meet and to go through details of how Patricia would work with Angela, as well as all other thoughts around the medical side of things.

At the lunch Patricia mentioned to us that we, as intended parents, were not actually her patients, but that Angela was, and therefore she would need to have a signed consent form from Angela in order for her to divulge any information pertaining to Angela or the pregnancy. This was not an issue but just a bit of bureaucracy that needed to be done.

Patricia also said that, as we were expecting twins, on the day they would be born we would only be allowed to have one father in the room with Angela, as there would be a lot of medical staff in the room, and two dads in the room would mean too many people. This of course brought up another decision that Steven and I had to make – which of us would be in the room. It really did not take us a long time to discuss it. We decided that, not only because I'm not very good with blood but also because Steven wanted our children to open their eyes at birth and be the first person that they ever saw, he would be the person to go into the room. More about this later on in this book because, as you will see, this very nearly was a decision that was taken out of our hands!

So back to the resort; we had an absolutely lovely weekend with Angela and her two boys. We spoke a lot with her and Patricia about Phoenix and her thoughts of the city, and where we should be looking to rent an apartment for after the babies were born. This was a big concern of mine as I didn't know Phoenix and therefore needed as much advice as possible.

We then spoke with the agency, because once you have chosen both the Ob–Gyn and the hospital in which the children were going to be born the agency should get in touch with them both just to run through logistics. Not only logistics, but actually also to lay the groundwork to make sure that there are no issues around a surrogate and two gay dads having children born in the hospital.

In our case, Patricia had said that if any of her staff were to have any sort of issue with two gay dads having children on her ward then they would not be on her staff, i.e. they would be made to leave! Always a good sign that she really was taking our side in this process. She even said that sometimes she gets comments that she always puts what her patients want first over what the nurses want her to do – at hearing that we really thought that we had found the most perfect person to deliver our babies!

In fact, we found out that our surrogacy agency makes multiple calls to the hospital, including to social workers and the registrar, in order to make sure that everyone is aware of the situation and that they know there will be more than the usual one mum and one dad with a child in the hospital post birth.

One thing that I think is normal for any birth is to ask if there are private rooms available pre and post birth, as well as a place for the intended parents to stay once the children have arrived. It could be that they don't have a private room available so you will need to find a hotel nearby. Thankfully in our case, the hospital had a room with an extra bed in it, so we ended up staying in the room with Angela.

The only potential problem that Patricia had was that she was scheduled to be on holiday the last week of August and the first two weeks of September, which could potentially conflict with when the twins could be born if they came early. Of course we didn't really pay much attention to that little detail until much later on in the process when we were worried that the twins might make an early appearance, but thankfully she managed to have her holiday and come back refreshed and raring to go in time for our children to make their guest appearance.

Questions to ask at this point

  a) Does your surrogate have her own Ob–Gyn that she would like to use?

b) Does your surrogate have a preference over which hospital she would like to have the children in?

c) Does that hospital have a history of dealing with surrogacy cases? If so, do they have a procedure in place that you can see? If not, ask your agency to get in touch and make sure that everyone is aware of the surrogacy arrangement.

d) Does your hospital have a NICU (neo-natal intensive care unit) that is part of the hospital in case anything goes wrong during the birth and the children need extra help?

e) Make sure that your surrogate signs paperwork with the Ob–Gyn in order that you are able to see all medical results.

f) Who would like to be in the room when the birth happens? Make sure that everyone involved on the day is ok with this.

g) Does the hospital have the facility for a private room before and after the birth for the surrogate?

h) Does the hospital have facilities for the intended parents, i.e. a room for you to stay in if you don't want to be with your surrogate, or is there a hotel that is close by?

15 DNA Testing

During the early to mid-pregnancy period, when there is not a lot to do apart from worry about how the pregnancy itself is going, you should start thinking about DNA testing and whether or not it is relevant to your situation.

Assuming, like in our family, that there are in fact two fathers and one mother, a very important part for the UK court process is obtaining DNA results for each of the children. If it is just one father and one mother then it isn't as big a deal, as the IVF clinic can prove which sperm source was the donor.

However, for the ability to apply for UK passports for the children it is necessary to have their citizenship deemed either 'UK citizenship by descent' (i.e. native UK father) or 'UK citizenship otherwise than by descent' (i.e. not-native UK Father). In our instance we have one of each of these two types as I am British and Steven is American with a visa to stay in the UK indefinitely. However, this unfortunately does not grant his child the right to a British passport – it just grants his child the ability to reside in the UK as long as he does. Make sure that you check at this time what the immigration laws are and how they apply to you – I would definitely consult with an immigration lawyer on this.

On top of the DNA test requirements for the passports, if you have told the hospital that there are two fathers then they will need the results in order to be able to identify who is the father of each child and have the correct father placed on the correct birth certificate. This is because in the US it is a crime to lie on a legal document (which a birth certificate is) and by filling in information that is not correct the person doing it could possibly end up in jail.

We used a company called EasyDNA to do this as they are

recognised by the judicial systems in both the US and the UK. Before the children were born we had paid an amount in the UK to the company and they sent through all of the required paperwork to our address in the UK. They then arranged for a local registered nurse to come to the hospital after the children were born in order to do swab testing on all of us.

The nurse actually also brought their own kit with her which we used in order to make sure that the chain of custody was intact. The whole process was in fact very simple, straightforward and painless. The nurse took a swab from each of our mouths with a very long cotton bud. She then did the same with each of the children. She placed each cotton bud in a plastic container and sealed them in an envelope which she then signed. We both filled in some forms, showed her some identification and she left.

She then took the envelopes and the forms and sent the tests away. We asked for the results to be expedited so that we would receive notarised results within 3 days (emailed first and then couriered to an address of our choosing).

It should be noted that the rule of chain of custody is highly important when doing DNA testing, and therefore it is really better if possible to pay extra and have the DNA company send in an independent tester to do everything so that you know it has been done properly.

Questions to ask at this point

a) Do you actually need to do DNA testing?
b) Does the hospital provide nurses to do the testing or do you want an external person to do it?
c) Do you want to expedite the results?
d) Can you ensure that the chain of custody is not broken?

16 Cord Blood Banking

One of the other things that we had thought about long before the twins were born was the ability to store the stem cells from the umbilical cord and the placenta. This is called cord blood and tissue banking, and we decided to go ahead with this for the simple reason that stem cells are the only cells in the body that can split and multiply into the building blocks of any part of the body.

Stem cells are prolific in the umbilical cord and placenta but, unfortunately, as we get older they disappear. Therefore, if for any reason down the line we needed to have them, we knew that we would be able to take them out of the cryo-storage where they are placed and use them. This typically is for things like leukaemia and other diseases and, although hopefully we will never need to use them, at least we have them.

In order to do this there is a straightforward process that needs to be followed. It is very easy to do, and as long as the obstetrician and their team are able to do it, then they will. In our case with the twins it was a 'nice-to-have'. However, if an emergency happened during the birthing process we decided (along with the obstetrician) that it would not be an issue if they didn't collect the stem cells.

We researched online for the different companies that offer this service and we found one that is also based in Arizona. The reason for this is that Arizona is actually quite quiet when it comes to things like natural disasters – there is no history of earthquakes, tornados or anything catastrophic that would affect a building that is storing millions and millions of cells. They do have a lot of fires, but thankfully not near the facility.

The company that we used is called Cord Blood Registry (CBR) and it is based in Tucson, Arizona. They were incredibly helpful in describing what needed to be done by the obstetrician, as well as by us on the days leading up to the birth.

You basically have to pay an upfront fee that covers the collection of the kits, processing of the stem cells and all the things that are needed for the first year of storage. Once they receive payment they will send you the pack that is required in the birthing room. We asked for the kits to be sent directly to the hospital as Patricia had agreed to look after them for us.

At this stage you will also need to fill out online enrolment forms, and you also will need to get your surrogate to fill out the same thing. This is a very simple procedure that needs everyone to sign in order that, going forward, you are able to access the stem cells without the need to contact the surrogate every time you want to discuss something with CBR.

For twins, the total cost for the first year, including all of the collection fees and figuring out how many stem cells were available, was just under $3,000. Then on an annual basis we will have to pay a storage fee, which currently stands at $150 per year. We have decided to keep these stem cells for as long as we can. I think that it is possible to donate them to science if at any stage you decide that you do not want to keep on paying the storage fee, or of course it is possible to just have them discarded.

After the babies were born we found out that the birth team had been able to collect blood from the umbilical cords and that it was ready to be sent by us to CBR. I felt a little bit like a vampire with blood bags in my hand as the packs were filled up with the cord blood – but thankfully the nurses had labelled everything properly and so we called the number on the back of the pack and a courier came to collect the pack and send it back to the company.

Bear in mind that this has to be done within 24 hours of the birth, but that is very easy to do as long as you remember to call the courier! Once the courier has taken the pack back to CBR, the company comes back to you to confirm receipt and let you know exactly how many cells were in the blood and have been frozen.

For those like me that are fascinated by biology, we retrieved 52cc of cord blood for Alexander which equates to a total of 439.79 million nucleated cells. For Liliana we retrieved slightly less at 31cc of cord blood which equates to 248.57 million nucleated cells.

Questions to ask at this point

a) Do you want to have the blood or the tissue from the umbilical cord / placenta stored?

b) If you do, make sure that everyone is aware of it and have the packs that you sent for ready during the birth.

17 Middle Pregnancy

Throughout the pregnancy I always had at the back of my mind all of the things that any pregnant couple worries about. What if something were to go wrong with the fertilisation process? Would the embryos actually take during the implantation stage? Would Angela get and remain pregnant? What if there were a problem with the babies? I guess that this is part of the emotional rollercoaster that every parent goes through during the pregnancy period – but that doesn't make it any easier! On top of that we had the initial worries of what if Angela decided that she didn't actually want to go through with the pregnancy and pulled out!

One of the things that Steven and I spoke about at length was the possibility of Down Syndrome with our children. We also spoke to Patricia about this as we were worried about our ages being a factor. She said that the reality was that because our egg donor was so young the probability of our embryos having Down Syndrome was very low.

Patricia reviewed all of the ultrasound scans as well as doing a nuchal translucency scan (which measures the amount of liquid at the back of the neck of the foetuses at 11 weeks). Her thoughts were that everything looked normal, and that it was an unnecessary step for Angela to undertake an amniocentesis test as the probability of Down Syndrome was very low to nil. Thankfully that was one of our worries removed.

Obviously we were completely unable to do anything about keeping Angela pregnant apart from hoping that she would be looking after herself by working out, eating well and making sure that she was taking her medication to keep her blood pressure within a normal range. We decided to keep the fact that we were pregnant very quiet from everyone during most of the pregnancy to avoid multiple questions, and it was only our closest family that we told at the 16-week mark.

Until about the 28-week mark we didn't buy anything for the children. I deep down think that this was because we really didn't believe that we were pregnant. With a surrogate thousands of miles away from us the whole process remained very surreal. One of the things about Angela being in the US and us in the UK was that we did not see the weekly changes in Angela's physical appearance as the babies were growing.

This physical distance was also very much an emotional distance too. In all honesty I'm not really sure how other people keep in touch with their surrogate during the pregnancy but after talking to Angela we decided to email her every second Thursday.

The first few months the emails were actually very brief, but as time went on Angela would tell us how she was doing physically and mentally. She also would email us with stuff that was going on in her life as she felt that this was also affecting the children and how she was doing things to make everything as positive an atmosphere as possible.

This was incredibly lovely of her to do but, to be honest, with the physical distance it was still very hard to stay connected with the reality of the pregnancy.

How one combats this is a very difficult subject. I think that this is a very personal discussion to have with your surrogate so that you are both on the same page. We didn't want to become a pain to Angela, but at the same time we really wanted to know what was going on so you have to find a balance that works for you all.

Questions to ask at this point

a) When do you want to start telling people that you are pregnant?

b) Would you like to have any medical procedures (amniocentesis) performed on the surrogate?

c) Is your contact with the surrogate too little, too much or ok? Find out if she thinks the same.

d) When do you want to start preparing the infrastructure that you are going to need once the babies arrive?

18 Healthcare Proxy Form

One thing that it is imperative to have when you get to the third trimester is a Healthcare Proxy form. This MUST be signed by the surrogate before she goes into hospital to give birth, and it is best to make a copy of it. Basically this is a form that entitles you, as the parents, access once the child has been born.

We didn't realise that this had to be done, but when Angela was admitted to the hospital I called the surrogacy agency to let them know. The person I spoke to said "oh, we have to send you through the healthcare proxy form now then". They sent me through a copy by email that Angela signed and I handed in to the nurse on duty.

Thankfully this wasn't a problem, but all I could think of is what would have happened if we had had an emergency situation and we didn't have this form.

I guess we would have then faced the situation where we were unable to visit our babies as the surrogate hadn't given her permission for us to be able to. Not ideal on any level!

This in my opinion was something that the surrogacy agency should have made sure months in advance that we had signed. After all they should have a check-list of everything that needs to be done and when something is completed then it should be ticked off thc list.

Question to ask at this point

a) Have you received your signed healthcare proxy form? If so, make a copy and make sure that the hospital has it on file.

19 Late Pregnancy

Unlike a singleton, which has a full term gestation period of 40 weeks, twins are considered full term at 37 weeks. Steven and I decided that it would be prudent for one of us to be on hand in Arizona a little bit early in case the twins decided to make an appearance before their 40 week due date of the 1st of October.

Therefore I flew out to the US on the 3rd September, which coincided with just after their 35th week of gestation, and settled in to the W Hotel in Scottsdale, where thankfully we had been upgraded from a normal room to a full on junior-suite. This was super lovely and only happened because the general manager found out what we were doing and upgraded us for the duration of our stay (potentially 4 weeks!).

Our friend Barbara, who was living in Texas at the time, decided (well I kind of blackmailed her into it) that she would come and keep me company whilst I was in Arizona. I persuaded her that we could spend some quality time together discovering Scottsdale, Phoenix and beyond.

Bearing in mind that we had really not bought much stuff for the babies this was an opportunity for me to sit down and start to figure out exactly what we were going to need. I had done some research in the UK and had put together a list of all of the different things you could think of for us to have to buy: cots, mattresses, prams, etc. The wonderful thing about the USA is that they have a mega-superstore called baby-r-us that has absolutely anything and everything that one could possibly want to do with a baby.

So there were Barbara and I on the morning of Friday 7th Sept, walking around a huge baby store, and I have to admit that I started to panic about the amount of stuff that one needs for a baby. It is insane to have to start thinking about baby nail clippers and hand mitts in case their nails are too long and they start scratching themselves. Or, how many different types of swaddles there are. Thankfully at this stage we had also arranged for Desiree, our maternity nurse, to join us, and she was a massive calming influence on me. We spent about 3 hours in the store and left with everything that we would need for our stay in the US.

Angela had an appointment on the Friday afternoon for another scan, so we joined her in the hospital and spent the afternoon watching and listening to the little ones' heart beats. The hospital told us that Angela would have to come back in on Tuesday morning in order to meet with Patricia, as she would be back from her holiday by then and wanted to see Angela.

So we spent the weekend enjoying the Arizona sun and sites and then on Tuesday 11th September in the morning we joined Angela and Patricia to go through with another ultrasound scan. Little did we know that everything was about to change in our lives.

Angela had her scan and Patricia then joined us in the room. She said that the boy was facing head down and that the girl was still in a breach position. In theory this was not such a big deal as it was possible that if the boy came out first then the girl could move position and come out head first. However, the concern that Patricia had was that Angela's blood pressure had started to rise and this, coupled with the girl's breach position, meant that she wanted to admit Angela into hospital and deliver the babies that afternoon.

EXCUSE ME! I nearly fell off my chair. Actually we all nearly did.

Patricia then continued her dialogue and said that it was her opinion that the safest medical way to deliver would be to plan a Caesarean section for Angela. That way they could be assured that the boy would be fine (he would have been a natural birth from his positioning) but that the girl would not get distressed during the labour.

Throughout the pregnancy Angela had said to us that she really wanted to have a natural birth as it was less intrusive on her body with a quicker recovery rate. As she had had two children naturally before, she didn't think it would be a problem. Obviously this was her choice, and as it was her body she was the one that was in the driving seat with any decisions around it.

In all honesty, we really would have preferred for her to have agreed up front to have a C-section. Not because we are 'too posh to push', but because it would enable us to plan all of the logistics around when the children were going to be born (i.e. flights, accommodation and rental car) in advance. When you are thousands of miles away, the ability to have things planned is massively stress reducing.

The other main reason for us wanting Angela to have a C-section was a medical one; with a planned operation, everyone who is supposed to have a role is there. The teams (of which there would be two as there were twins) of people that are required to be in the room are all prepared in advance, there are no last minute hitches and everyone is on the same page.

My understanding is that when a natural birth turns into an emergency C-section it is a mad panic at the last minute to make sure everything is in order, and that could lead to complications. And unnecessary stress!

Anyway, back to the hospital and, a testament to the amazing woman that Angela is, she asked Patricia what, in her medical opinion, was the best thing for the babies. Patricia said she thought a C-section was the best thing and Angela looked at me, smiled, and said if that was the best thing for the babies then that is what she would do.

At this stage I started having a very real panic – Steven was still in the UK and they wanted us to have the babies that day. There was absolutely no way that he would be able to make the flight to Phoenix in time for later that afternoon, especially as there is only one direct flight a day and that is on a British Airways flight that had already left London.

So I asked Patricia if it would be possible to hold off the C-section until the next day when Steven could hopefully fly in on time to be there. She said that it would be possible, but that they would still have to admit Angela and put her on 24-hour monitoring to make sure that her blood pressure did not become dangerous for her or the babies. If it did, then they would have to deliver the babies. She also told me to get hold of Steven and fly him out to the US as soon as possible.

So I called Steven to tell him the news, but he didn't pick up his mobile phone. I kept on calling him and after 2 hours managed to get hold of him – he'd been in a meeting with his phone on silent!!! As soon as I got hold of him he said, "By the 74 missed calls I'm assuming we're having the babies!…" Got it in one.

Steven had his flight booked for the following Saturday, but we were now having to fly him over 4 days early. We had prepared for this eventuality by buying a flexible ticket from British Airways as the only carrier to fly direct at the time from London to Phoenix. However, the only day that they do not fly out is on a Wednesday, which just happened to be the next day!

So then we had to figure out how we were going to get him to Phoenix. British Airways were pretty good at figuring out the first flight that he could get on, which left Heathrow at 9 a.m. for Dallas. Then he could get American Airlines from Dallas to Phoenix… BUT … the flexible ticket we had bought didn't actually give us the flexibility that we needed. We had to pay the difference in fare and the only ticket available (surprise, surprise) was in First Class … oh, and that would be another £7,000 on top of the £6,000 we'd already spent on the ticket!

You can imagine exactly what we thought and, in fact, said at the time, but what could we do? Either Steven didn't make the birth of our children or he paid it and he was there. Thanks to the joy of a credit card, we reluctantly paid the money and booked him on the flight.

Questions to ask at this point

a) Have you thought about the logistics of getting to the US in time for the birth?

b) Have you got all of the stuff that you will need for when the baby arrives?

c) Where are you going to stay up to and after the birth, and do you need a rental car?

d) If you are having a maternity nurse, is she on call in case the baby arrives early?

20 The Birth

So, there we were, in a hospital room all to ourselves, Angela, Barbara and me all kind of in shock at the fact that we were going to have the babies the next day. I'm pretty good when it comes to things like having blood taken, and I'm not really that squeamish, but the nurse came in and inserted a saline drip into the top of Angela's right hand, took one look at me turning green and asked if I needed to go and get some air! Yes, please … off I went for a walk.

In all honesty I was in a state of shock – I knew all along that this moment was going to arrive, but it really started to sink in that we were going to be parents the next day! I wonder if every parent goes through the enormity of this at this time. I would assume so. All of a sudden the reality of bringing another child into the world, the fact that they will be utterly dependent on you for, arguably, the next 20 years is huge. The next generation was about to arrive!

I went back to the hospital room and the nurses had put a monitoring machine on Angela, which basically meant that she had a blue strap and a pink strap wrapped around her belly, one with a monitor on the boy and one with a monitor on the girl. Both were turned on and we could hear the little heart beats of both of them. The sound on the machines was only turned on for a few minutes at a time, but every time it was turned on Angela's blood pressure started to drop down to normal levels, so we asked the nurses to keep the machines turned on so that the noise could be beneficial to Angela's blood pressure.

Angela started dozing on and off whilst Barbara and I kept looking at each other with that look of shock on both of our faces. Thank the Lord that Barbara was there to keep me company, as otherwise I really don't know what I would have done.

We had a great Italian meal from a local restaurant and then Angela sent Barbara and me home for what she said would be "My last night of sleep for a while!" If only I could sleep – we were about to become a family, moving from two people to four and, yes, I was incredibly emotional, stressful and filled with trepidation about what was going to happen the next day.

Eventually I fell asleep, but then Steven called me to tell me he was boarding the plane to Dallas and he had not slept at all – he and my best friend had been up all night talking about the babies and how our lives were going to change, and they had polished off a few bottles of wine in the process. Allegedly it was to help him sleep on the plane, but I know he was just as nervous as I was. So he boarded his flight and I go back to sleep, and when he landed in Dallas it was still only 9 a.m. in Arizona. He then had to sit and wait in Dallas airport until his connecting flight, which was scheduled to land at Phoenix airport at 3.20 p.m.

Barbara and I made our way over to the hospital the following morning via Dunkin Donuts. Someone once told me that the nurses in the maternity ward are always overlooked, as once the baby actually arrives everyone and everything else is forgotten about. So I bought 24 donuts (with a huge coffee for me), and we made our way through to the maternity and delivery ward.

As you can imagine, the nurses who had done a night shift loved the 22 donuts (one had of course jumped into my mouth and one into Barbara's mouth), and the ones that were joining for their day shift could not believe their luck – they were getting a sugar high before they had even started their day – a great success all round. Selfishly, I also wanted them to remember us just in case we needed anything to be done.

Patricia came around later on in the morning, as she was going to be delivering some children, and checked with me that Steven was definitely on his way. The wonderful thing about American Airlines (which was actually who Steven ended up flying with due to the code-sharing agreement) is that you are able to track the flight online so we could see exactly where he was at every stage.

In fact, it became a bit of a running joke with the nurses, who kept asking me which state he was flying over (I'm English, I don't know!!) at different times during the day. He finally landed at Phoenix Airport at 3.28 p.m., got a taxi to the hospital, which was 10 minutes away, and walked into our room at the delivery ward at 4 p.m. You can imagine the sigh of relief (and admittedly a few tears on my behalf) that he was finally there.

One of the nurses came in and asked Angela if she would like to have a shower before the operation, as afterwards she would be in bed for a few days. She jumped at the chance to do that, and we went to get a coffee. We then had some time together with Barbara and Angela, catching up, before finally Patricia came in and said, "It's show time, boys and girls".

As I've mentioned before, Steven had immediately volunteered to be in the room with Angela when the babies were born as he wanted to be the first person that they saw when they first opened their eyes. So, with my ability to turn green at the sight of blood and the fact that he had made it to the US in time, Steven was told to put on a white hospital gown over his clothes and they asked Angela to get into a wheelchair. At 4.20 p.m. we all walked with her from the room that we had to the door leading in to the operating room.

Obviously had he not have been able to make it in time then I would have definitely been in the room with Angela, but as he was now there Barbara and I could go back to our room and sit and await the children's arrival to the world. PHEW. All I could now worry about was if everything was going to be OK, and whether or not Steven would remember to take photos on the camera I had shoved into his hands.

On Wednesday 12ᵗʰ September our children were born at 37 weeks into their gestation period. Alexander came out at 5.28 p.m. weighing 6 lbs 6 oz with a shock of dark black hair, and Liliana came out at 5.30 p.m. weighing 5 lbs 15 oz with a very light blond fuzz. They were both around 50 cm tall, which meant that Angela had been carrying 1 metre of baby – something to this day that I still find incredible!

Finally, a nurse came to the room where we were waiting nervously and told Barbara and I to follow her. We walked through to the Neonatal Intensive Care Unit (NICU), where it was routine for twins to be put overnight, and I was shown our babies. More tears, hugs and a lot of little finger holding of the new additions to our family.

Eventually Angela was wheeled back into her room and we went to join her. We decided that, as she had done so much for us and given us such an amazing gift, the least we could do was to stay with her in the room, so we took it in turns to spend the next 3 night with her on the fold-out bed.

A C-section is a major operation and therefore Angela had nurses coming in throughout the night to check on her to see if she was ok, as well as doing lots of monitoring of her blood pressure, etc. In the morning Patricia came in and said that Angela had in fact had a very rough night medically, and that was why they kept coming in so often. Thankfully she spent the next day recovering very well.

During the next few days that we were in the hospital we had an amazing array of staff come in and view the babies. Everyone was so incredibly helpful that we really did feel that we were part of the family. I think that this was down to two things: 1) I am not sure if they had ever had two gay dads from the UK in their hospital before, and 2) as we were on such a high we were continually being really nice to everyone. It's amazing how a smile and a thank you can change someone from being busy and grumpy to happy and helpful.

We took a shine to one of the nurses in the hospital, Sarah, who was just wonderful. Having battled breast cancer, and also as a mum of 5 herself, there was nothing that phased her and nothing that was too much trouble. As she was temporary relief staff we asked her if the following week she would be free to work for us and to look after Angela whilst she recovered at home from the operation. Thankfully Sarah was in fact free and agreed to drive daily to Angela's house to make sure that she was recovering from her operation as expected.

Angela is the kind of woman who believes that she never needs any help and that her role in life is to help others. We felt that for once in her life she should have someone to come in and look after her, even if just to do the chores, especially as she had just had a serious operation and realistically she did need to be helped.

After a C-section a woman should not lift things, should not really overexert herself and should ideally spend time in bed resting. As a mother of two boys we knew that Angela would do all of the things that she should not be doing, and therefore having Sarah around was of great help. Some have said that what we did was over and above what we should have done, but in reality we felt that Angela had given us such an amazing gift that this was the least we could do.

During this whole period we were of course busy looking after the children – we kept them in the same room as Angela in order that she could spend some time with them. We felt that would aid in her healing from the C-section. At the same time as looking after the little ones we also had to start dealing with the mass of bureaucracy around the birth certificates.

Questions to think of at this point

a) Have you thought about something for the staff looking after your surrogate before the baby arrives? Donuts are a classic choice.

b) Are you going to have photographs/video taken of the birth?

c) If your surrogate is going to have a C-section, does she have the support network in place at home to help her with all of the things that she will not be able to do?

21 US Birth Orders and Birth Certificates

One thing that was not really explained fully at the time of choosing our surrogate was the importance about pre- and post-birth orders. Or maybe it was but, as you have probably noticed by now, there are so many decisions going on at the same time it is so easy to lose track!

In a nutshell, a pre-birth order is a court order telling the registrar (the person legally registering the birth of the babies) to put the two dads on the birth certificate, i.e. the birth mother waives her right to having her name on the birth certificate **before** the babies are born.

A post-birth order is the same thing but done **after** the birth happens. There are some states in the US that do not allow pre-birth orders to be issued, in other states you have to be state resident to get a pre-birth order, and then in other states it is open for anyone to obtain.

In the instance of a post-birth order, a birth certificate is issued with the birth mother on it and then, at some date after the birth of the child, an attorney goes to the court and files paperwork that requests for the fathers to be included on the birth certificate and for the birth mother to be removed.

It should be noted that, in the case of there being only one father, then that person is able to go on the birth certificate at the time of birth. Once the order is granted in the courts, the birth mother can then be removed from the birth certificate.

We were not told that Arizona is one of the states in which a pre-birth order cannot be given unless you are an Arizona resident… So it well-worth asking your surrogacy agency the question of whether or not pre-birth orders are able to be done in the state before signing up the surrogate. However, there is a downside to having a pre-birth order granted. I've mentioned it before but (to reiterate as it is a very important point) if one is obtained and the fathers go on the birth certificate at birth, then the babies are unable to go on the birth mother's insurance. They are now dependents of the fathers and she no longer has anything to do with the children in the eyes of the healthcare world.

To obtain the orders (both pre- and post-) one needs to go via an attorney in the particular state the surrogate resides and where the babies are born. That attorney will then fill out all of the required paperwork that you and the surrogate will be required to sign, and then they will file them in the court.

It is probably best to have all of the paperwork done whilst in the attorney's office because all of the signatures need to be notarised and the attorney can present the documents to the court. We didn't do that, and then found when we went to get the documents notarised at a bank (as they are able to do it) that not every bank would recognise a UK passport as a means of identification – not quite sure why, but they didn't.

For us, the process was such that the registrar put Angela on the birth certificate as the mother but, because we didn't have the DNA records yet, we were unable to put any fathers on. If you have the ability to expedite the DNA testing, and you have the results with you, then the registrar should be able to put the correct father on the birth certificate there and then along with the surrogate (who even though she is not the genetic mother is the birth mother and thus goes on the birth certificate). If, however, the DNA results are going to take time, as in our case, you have to wait.

Once we received back the notarised DNA results in paper form we went to the Vital Records office and filled in the paperwork to get the respective fathers added to the birth certificates. When both mother and father are going to be on the birth certificate (pre-birth singleton), I would recommend asking for about four or five copies, as one never knows how many birth certificates one needs and later on down the line it might be quite painful to obtain copies.

If, as for us, there are two fathers and one mother and you are doing the paperwork post-birth, then it is worthwhile asking the attorney to get in touch with Vital Records before you go to collect the birth certificates. This fills them in on the situation so that it doesn't come as a surprise that there are two dads.

In our case, as we didn't know that it was a good idea, we spent all day in the Vital Records office waiting for the clerk to talk to his superiors, who in turn had to talk to the Attorney General to approve a birth certificate with the surrogate and one father on one birth certificate and the other father on the other. Just painful and totally avoidable!

Once the birth certificates with the surrogate and the respective fathers on had been issued, we then went back to the attorney and got him to apply to the courts for the surrogate to be removed – this is a process that takes a couple of weeks. Basically the surrogate is again legally waiving her parental responsibility rights in front of the US Courts, and this means that she can be removed from the birth certificate. For us, this process took about 3 weeks to complete.

Also, at the time of birth you can apply for a social security number (SSN) for your baby. The registrar at the hospital did this for us at the same time as registering the twins' births. She asked which address we would like the SSN to be sent to and we gave my in-law's address. It can take up to 12 weeks to issue the SSN, so if you don't have a permanent address in the US then maybe ask the surrogate if she would be willing to forward the documentation on to you.

Why is it important to have a SSN? Basically your child will need it if they ever want to work in the US. It is also required to collect benefits or to receive any other government services. On top of this, most US institutions require it as a secondary form of identification, i.e. banks. Therefore if you want your child to have the option of living in the US it is just one less thing to have to think about in the future.

Questions to ask at this point

a) Is the state in which your surrogate based a pre-birth or a post-birth order state?

b) Does your attorney need to contact Vital Records to notify them that you are coming in and that the children are the result of surrogacy?

c) Do you want a social security number for your child?

d) Where will you be sending the social security card?

22 Baby Routine

So, fast forward to the weekend after the babies were born and we finally left the hospital. Desiree greeted us at the hotel where we were staying overnight and we became a family for the next few weeks. She made sure that all of the new clothes that we had bought for the babies were washed and ironed, ready to be used, and then she got to work being the maternity nurse.

Luckily we had been offered a house to stay in that belonged to an old friend of Steven's in a city north of Phoenix called Sedona. It is actually idyllic and the house is absolutely stunning. We were given the most perfect spot in order for us all to relax into becoming a family!

Desiree's routine centres around the babies having a 3-hour cycle: that means that basically every 3 hours the children are fed, cleaned and played with until they fall asleep again. Obviously as they get older the amount of time they are awake gets longer, but in the first few days it was so funny trying to wake up the babies so that they would eat. We even resorted to dipping their feet in the swimming pool to wake them up (and even that didn't work sometimes).

As the weeks progressed, Desiree dropped the night feeds so that the children stopped having a 4 a.m. feed, then stopped having the 1 a.m. feed and eventually stopped having the 10 p.m. feed. At this stage the children were 10 weeks old, and they were now eating everything that they needed to eat during the day and literally sleeping from 7 p.m. until 7 a,m.

I have attached in Appendix 3 the routine that we used and still used up until the babies were about 6 months old. Obviously, up until we stopped giving the children their night feeds we kept on doing the 3-hourly cycle, just with no play time at 1 a.m. and 4 a.m. In the middle of the night we fed them and then let the babies go back to sleep. Well, when I say we, it was actually Desiree that did all of the hard night shifts. For the first few weeks of the babies' life they slept in the same room as Desiree and she did all of the night feeding. Therefore it is true to say that the only time I've had to get up in the middle of the night to feed my children was when they were in the hospital straight after they were born. Absolute bliss and well worth every penny we spent.

For family reasons we ended up asking Desiree to stay on for a few extra weeks and to help us through to when the children were 10 weeks old. So she actually flew back with us to the UK and adjusted the babies to their new time-zone. Although this leads me on to the next major thing to go through – immigration!

23 UK Immigration

One of the most important bureaucratic parts of the process that we also didn't really understand at the beginning of the whole surrogacy journey is the part surrounding the paperwork for bringing our children back to the UK.

Assuming that you want your babies to have US citizenship, the first thing you have to do is to get the babies their US passports. Once the babies are born and you have the birth certificates in hand you can start this application process.

There are many ways to apply for US passports, and a list of all of the information that you need to provide can be found on the Bureau of Consular Affairs website, which currently is www.travel.state.gov/passport. You can also do it in some post offices, or you can use an 'expediter' service.

In our instance we opted to use an expediter service that offered services from a 1-day turnaround to a 1-month turnaround. The cost for using the expediter service ranges from about $300 for the 1–3-day turnaround to $100 for the 2-week turnaround.

We filled out all of the forms online and then arranged to go to an 'acceptance agent' (which could in fact also be the post office that I've mentioned above) in order to verify that all of the documentation we put together was valid. You also have to appear in person with the children and sign all of the documents in front of the acceptance agent, otherwise they will not allow the paperwork to go through.

Once you have their US passport, you then have a choice to make about how you are going to come back to the UK. Assuming that you are a UK citizen, then your child is entitled to a UK passport (obviously there are rules around who is entitled and who isn't), which then presents three options for coming back to the UK:

1. on a US tourist visa with a US passport
2. on an entry visa with a US passport
3. with a UK passport.

The option you take will be determined by numerous factors relevant to your situation. I would think that people will predominantly take route 1, as the time it takes to do either option 2 or 3 can potentially add weeks to the process and you will have to remain in the US for all of that time. In 2013, according to the UK border agency website, 95% of applications were processed within 12 weeks of the settlement application and 100% of cases within 24 weeks of application.[2]

However, with option 1 you run the risk of being turned away at UK border control as you are breaking the tourist visa rules – you are entering the UK with a child that has the intention of overstaying their 6-month tourist visa; so this is the riskiest way of coming into the UK and not one that I would recommend.

With options 2 and 3 you are dealing with a lot of bureaucracy and you do not want to get it wrong. I would really suggest that you get in touch with an immigration lawyer to walk you through all of the options that are open to you and to see how much it will cost for them to do the process.

Also, options 2 and 3 will involve a lot more paperwork and online applications, as well as potentially turning up in person at the UK Embassy in the US, but these are the safest (and legal) ways to come into the UK. So that you are able to see the complexity of the visa situation, and what needs to be done, the website that has all of the information required on how to apply for a visa is www.ukba.homeoffice.gov.uk/countries/usa/applying

Looking back on it now, we really did not understand all of the implications and timelines of the options available and the reality is that we should have had this explained to us, but we did not speak with an immigration lawyer and we took option 1. As Steven is American and I am British we thought that logically it would be ok for us to do this. I now know that actually it was a very risky route for us to take!

In all honesty this is one of the parts of the whole process where I now feel that maybe we should have engaged the services of an immigration lawyer. But one lives and learns.

Questions to ask at this point

a) Do you want your child to get a US passport?
b) How are you going to get your child their US passport – expediter or normal route?
c) Have you spoken with an immigration lawyer about bringing your child back to the UK?

.

24 Travel Document From Surrogate

Before you part ways with the surrogate you must get her to sign a travel consent form in front of your attorney in the US and then get the attorney to notarise it. We got Angela to do this at the same time that she was signing all of the court papers for the post-birth order application. It in essence gives you, as the parents, the right to travel without her being there. The wording that we used for this form is in Appendix 4 – your US lawyer will draw up something very similar, but I included it here just in case you want to compare and contrast.

Most airlines will ask to see a document if only one parent is travelling with the children in order to make sure that the children are not being abducted/removed from the country without the other parent's consent. I have heard that some airlines have refused travel without this document, so it is a 'good to have'.

I would also have each father do the same, allowing the other father to travel with the babies just in case only one of you is travelling with the children. We did this and, although we were not asked for it by the British Airways check-in staff at the airport, one never knows if they will ask for it or not.

For the actual form, we took the wording from the surrogate's travel consent form and amended it so that it was Father 1 giving permission for Father 2 to travel with the children. You can do this yourself and then have it notarised, which will save you some legal fees and maybe some hassle in the airport!

Question to ask at this point

    a)   Have you got a notarised travel consent form?

25 Finally Home

So here we were back in the UK, and all of a sudden the reality of having children hit us. Whilst we were in the US it was almost like we were on holiday with someone else's children, and I guess we felt that once we were back home life would return to what it was like beforehand. How wrong we were.

First of all, the thing that we should have really thought about beforehand was would one of us stay at home or would we both go back to work? If one of us was going to be at home, then who was it going to be? Anyway, we hadn't discussed it. We're both self-employed, but Steven is currently busier than me, so by natural default that meant I would be the stay-at-home dad.

We always knew that we were going to get a female nanny to act as a balancing female influence for the children (more about her in a bit). And the reality is that, with having a full-time nanny, neither of us needed to stay at home during the day, but we thought it best for the children to have a stable father role in their lives from day 1 – a dad who was around all day long from the minute they woke up to the minute they went to sleep.

However, this in itself then brings up a whole host of issues as, being self-employed, if I don't work then I don't earn any money. Therefore, if I am not working and bringing in my own money, do I all of a sudden have to start asking Steven for money, something that I'd never done as I've always been very self-sufficient? And is it just expected that, as the care-giver, I'm going to be the one that has to pay for everything to do with the children?

This in itself is worthy of a very long discussion between couples, as it's a very emotional topic involving a lot of figuring out of who is going to do what. The reality is that every couple is different, and I can't really give you advice on it as what your situation is will never be the same as the person next to you, or even the person next to them. So you have to talk about it – communication as always is key – to ascertain who is going to do what.

Believe me, shopping for twins is an incredibly expensive exercise every time I leave the house! In fact just the amount of clothes that they go through, as well as shampoo, baby wash, body moisturiser and nappies, is crazy. On top of that, the quantity of food that they eat is mind-boggling, and with a tub of baby formula costing around £10 your cash run-rate is rather large. Then again, this is nothing new to those people who have had a family for a while, but to us it was a massive surprise.

As I've mentioned before, on top of the daily stuff there is of course all of the paraphernalia that goes along with having babies: high chairs, car seats, cots, walkers, bath seats… In fact the list is endless, as at every stage of their little lives they need extra things. Thankfully we were given a lot of stuff by siblings and friends, but we still needed to buy a lot of things.

In Appendix 2 I have included a list that our maternity nurse sent to us before the children were born. It really is a very comprehensive list of pretty much everything that you could possibly need in the first few weeks. What I would suggest is that you buy stuff as you need it, as that way you do not end up over buying and having a lot of things that you never use. This will hopefully reduce your initial outlay.

At this stage, and on the advice of many people including our maternity nurse, we also employed a full-time nanny. She works for us from Monday to Friday, and from around 10 a.m. until 7 p.m., and frankly is a life-saver. Using Desiree's routine we do not need a night-nurse as the children go to sleep at 7 p.m. and then don't wake up until the following morning.

There is something about having an impartial person to be able to help out when you're exhausted or need to meet up with people, or frankly to be able to say, "This one smells of poo" and to have them take the children off your hands and change them. I'm not averse to changing nappies, but after a while being able to get someone else to do it is just wonderful!

If we didn't have the ability to hire our nanny then we would have muddled our way through having twins and everything that entails. However, if it is financially possible then I would recommend anyone that has twins to get some form of external help, as it will save your sanity.

For our nanny, we use a great agency that takes care of all of the tax side of things for her. They send me her pay slips every month, as well as letting us know the quarterly amount of tax and national insurance (social security contribution) that we have to pay for her. This service costs about £200 a year but is well worthwhile, as figuring out tax for someone else is rather complicated.

Obviously we are very lucky to be able to afford her. If, in your case, it isn't financially possible, then you just have to make sure that you are asking everybody and anybody to lend a helping hand. Lots of people are willing to come and help play with the children, but even with a nanny I ask friends who are popping in to stop in at the supermarket and get some food, milk, nappies or anything we need.

We recently had friends come and stay with us, and the wonderful thing about having them for the weekend was that whilst we were doing bath and bed time they were making supper, setting the table and getting everything ready for when the little ones went to bed. That was just absolutely amazing.

I say this because, in the first few months, you won't even have the time to really do anything. Sounds like I'm exaggerating, but as you are getting used to having children and adapting your life around them it is just all rather full-on and manic. I remember there were a few days when I would feel that there were only two times a day when I had 30 minutes to myself. One was at around noon when I would finally get in the shower, and the second time was at 4 p.m. when they were asleep and I wasn't preparing lunch or supper or washing clothes. Just crazy!

Thankfully, the craziness diminishes as you all adapt to the new routine, but it's definitely a shock to the system. Although I do have a feeling that at every step of the way there is some form of craziness, and that it is constantly mixed with an anxiety of sorts. In fact, I have a feeling that this is called being a parent.

Then, on top of that, there is working at your own relationship with your partner. In our situation, Steven works incredibly hard, which obviously entails many hours in the office, and there are definitely times when I resent him not being at home helping me with the children. This is completely unfair and I know it, as he really does his fair share of looking after the children when he's with them – in fact he does more than his fair share, I just wish he were here all the time. Then again, I guess this is the classic conundrum of one parent at home with the children all week long wishing the other was there too.

I have also turned into a bit of a cliché, as sometimes if he has a work dinner or drinks I catch myself saying, "I'm at home with the babies, and you go out and enjoy yourself". When did I turn into that person? I mean, seriously, how unreasonable is that!! I can, in fact, pinpoint when I changed – it was when we had babies.

Prepare yourself that your life is going to be completely different to how it was before and, no matter how strong your relationship was before they arrived, you will argue at times with your other half. In fact, someone once told me that any couple should really try their utmost not to divorce in the first year after having a child – I can see why they gave that very sage advice … it's so true. You just have to figure out all of the things that need to be done whilst at the same time you really must desperately try to be nice to each other.

The other piece of advice that I was given is to make time for a date night with your other half. I definitely felt that the first few months we were just fire-fighting the whole time, and in all honesty we were too tired to even thing about going out or in fact to do anything in the evenings. On top of that I didn't want to go out and leave someone that I didn't really think was capable of looking after our children in our house. However, I really think that this piece of advice is a very important thing to do.

In fact, we found that as time passes (and for us the seminal date was once the children had reached 6 months old) we really didn't mind getting a baby-sitter in for an evening every few weeks so that we could go and reconnect with our friends. That, and we are also now definitely making the most of having friends come over to help with bath and feeding time and then staying for supper afterwards. It's a new form of socialising, but it seems to be working for us at the moment. In fact, it is amazing how one learns how to relax around the children after a while.

Questions to ask at this point

a) Which of you (if at all) is going to be the stay-at-home parent?

b) Have you discussed thoroughly the financial aspects of who is going to be paying for what with regards the children, i.e. food, clothing, schooling?

c) Do you want to buy the infrastructure that you need upfront or do you want to figure it out as you go along?

d) Are you going to employ a nanny?

e) Are you willing to start going on date-nights with your partner?

26 UK Court Process

Anyway, enough about my life and more about the bureaucratic process that you still have to keep on top of.

Once Angela had extinguished all of her rights in the US we thought that we would be recognised worldwide as the parents, and therefore we would be the people able to make decisions on behalf of the children. However, this is not actually the case in the UK. I didn't even realise that we would have to go through any form of process in the UK, but the reality is that if you don't then the children, although legally yours in the eyes of the US, are not entirely yours in the eyes of the UK system.

To be recognised as the people entitled to make decisions for the children we needed to get a Parental Responsibility Order (which I refer to as the Parental Order). This is a UK court-ordered document giving you the responsibility to provide a home for and to protect and maintain a child. In the UK, the birth mother automatically receives this parental responsibility but the father does not (unless the father is married to the birth mother, which blatantly we are not).

This is, in reality, a straightforward process, but it is very bureaucratic and of course by definition a very legal procedure. A lot of people use lawyers to do the whole process for them as it is very daunting, but we decided that, being intelligent human beings, we should be able to do the UK court process ourselves, as it is not a legal requirement to have a lawyer or a barrister present.

There are multiple surrogacy lawyers in the UK and I would highly recommend that you have a look at anyone that you feel a connection with and talk to them. Depending upon when you approach the lawyer, they should walk you through the surrogacy process from a

UK legal perspective and then detail how they are going to be able to help you with your journey. Bear in mind the costs can range from a few thousand pounds up to £35,000 or more. This is definitely something that is not part of the surrogacy agency's remit and so they are not able to inform you of costs but you should be aware now that it could add a significant amount of money to the total you could spend.

A VERY important point at this juncture is that the Parental Order paperwork **MUST** be submitted within 6 months of the baby being born otherwise, under UK law, the Parental Order cannot be applied for – this is something that is non-negotiable! It doesn't have to be completed within 6 months, just submitted.

Therefore, as soon as we arrived back to the UK I went online and printed out the C-51 Application for a Parental Order form, which is part of the Section 54 of the Human Fertilisation and Embryology Act 2008[3] the "Act".

I read the Act fully and thought that our surrogacy process was relatively straightforward and that we actually ticked most of the boxes required to be granted a Parental Order. The boxes that need ticking are in Appendix 1, but in a nutshell they are:

- The child was born as a result of IVF
- The applicants are a couple living together
- The genetic material from one of the IPs has been used to make the baby
- The child lives with the applicants at the time of the Parental Order application
- The applicants are UK domiciled at the time of the Parental Order application
- The application was made freely
- Both applicants are over 18.

---

[3] http://www.legislation.gov.uk/ukpga/2008/22/section/54

One crucial box that isn't listed above is that we would need to explain why we paid our surrogate a fee to carry the twins. Remember that commercial surrogacy is illegal in the UK and in essence intended parents are not allowed to pay a surrogate more than reasonable expenses!

It is worthwhile making sure that you can tick all of the boxes. This saves a lot of time and money if you are not eligible to obtain a Parental Order. The biggest exception to this (which didn't apply to us) is that if you are a single intended parent then you are not able to apply for a Parental Order. A single person has to share the parental responsibility with the surrogate!

A friend asked us what the point was in applying for the Parental Order route, as it is a long legal process, but the reasons I've discovered are:

- If you get divorced then you both have rights over the child – with no Parental Order then the biological dad has rights and not the other dad
- If you die and have a natural child then the child via surrogacy is deemed an equal – with no Parental Order they could be cut out of any Will.

I'm sure there are other reasons, but these two were enough for us. So I filled out the C-51 application and took it to the Inner London Family Proceedings Court, which in 2012 was located at 59-65 Wells Street, London, W1A 3AE, and I submitted the paperwork to the legal clerks there.

At the time of our application a singleton parental order application cost £200. As we were doing a joint application with children who shared the same mother they viewed the twins as a single application, and so we only had to pay the fee of £200.

Over the next few weeks the Family Court department that was set up to deal with the welfare of children, CAFCASS[4], reviewed the C-

51 application and, as it was an international surrogacy case, they referred our application up to the High Court, where it was then submitted to be reviewed by a Senior High Court Judge. Sounds all very official and daunting – which to us it was!

CAFCASS also at the same time appointed a Parental Order Reporter (for all intents and purposes a social worker) who came to our house to interview us and to see the surroundings in which the children would be growing up. Bear in mind all officials involved in this process have to determine what is in the best interest of the child. In our case, the Parental Order Reporter called me up and made an appointment to come and meet up with us on the 14th February 2013.

In the week before her visit we started wondering exactly what the person coming to see us would ask us, what they would think and also what power did they have? Would they be able to take the children away from us and put them in social care? Of course, our anxiety levels started rising, but when she turned up she could not have been nicer.

I can't remember everything that she asked us during our meeting, but it lasted for about 3 hours and in that time she asked us questions around surrogacy and points pertaining to the Act. As I've mentioned under Section 54 you must make sure that you tick all of the points in Appendix 1 otherwise the High Court will not be able to grant you a Parental Order, so this is what she was doing.

The questions she asked included information on:

- Why we had decided to have children via surrogacy and not via adoption

---

4 The **Children and Family Court Advisory and Support Service (CAFCASS)** is a non-departmental public body for England and Wales [1] set up to safeguard and promote the welfare of children involved in family court proceedings - http://en.wikipedia.org/wiki/Children_and_Family_Court_Advisory_and_Suppo rt_Service

- Why we had chosen the US over the UK
- Our family network and how they are involved with the children
- Our day-to-day support network (she also met our nanny)
- How much we had paid the surrogate and did we have any documentation from the agency to show the payments made
- Our civil partnership certificate and our birth certificates.

Finally, she wanted to meet the children and see them in their environment (bedroom, playroom, kitchen, etc.)

During the meeting we made photocopies of a lot of the documentation for her. When she left she said that she would be writing a report on everything and that her report would then be sent through the CAFCASS network to the Senior High Court Judge in charge of our case.

A few weeks later you should receive a letter from the Family Court with a date on it for you to go to the Principal Family Registry Division, i.e. the High Court section for family issues. Make sure that the Parental Order Reporter is aware of the day that you are going to the court, as it could be that they are able to attend. Ours said that she would try to come but that, as she was very busy, it was not guaranteed that she would be able to.

As I mentioned, we did the whole court process ourselves but at the same time I was worried that maybe we were doing something incorrectly. As our court date approached I spoke to Louisa Ghevaert, who is one of the top surrogacy lawyers in the UK; as Louisa and I had met previously with work connected to CT Fertility I asked her what more I needed to prepare. She is just wonderful and sent me a list of more things that I needed to put together in duplicate (one for me, one for the court) and to hand in to the courts.

At the same time she said that if things started to go a bit awry then to give her a call and she would work for us on an hourly basis to complete the application. She continued by saying that she has the whole spectrum of clients – those that want her to do absolutely everything for them in order to get the legal process sorted and those like us who were doing it themselves but needed guidance and everything in between.

Louisa also said that it was very important for us to go to the hearings with the children so that the Judge would be able to see us a family unit and see how we interact together.

She also said that I should really have submitted all of the below paperwork with the original application but, as I hadn't, to take it with me to the hearing. So in two folders, organised in different sections as per the numbers below, I included originals in one file and copied documents in another:

1. C-51 applications, CAFCASS correspondence and all responses etc.
2. Surrogacy agency agreement signed by all parties
3. Surrogacy contract signed by all parties
4. Egg donor contract signed by all parties
5. Surrogate profile information (psychological evaluation and her application to be a surrogate)
6. Details of payments made to the surrogacy agency and, via escrow, those made to the surrogate
7. Notarised letter from the surrogate saying that she has no objection to the intended parents being granted the Parental Order – this must be dated **AFTER** 6 weeks of the birth of the babies for it to be relevant under UK law
8. A statement from us on why we chose international surrogacy, etc.
9. Our civil partnership certificate
10. Copies of our passports
11. A letter from our US attorney stating that what we had done was in compliance with Arizona state law
12. Application for US Parenting Orders and Parental Orders
13. The order from the US Court granting us all parental rights

14. Letter from IVF clinic stating that they had used gametes from the intended parents
15. US birth certificates with and without the surrogate's names on
16. US passports for the babies
17. DNA results – notarised.

Bear in mind that Angela is unmarried, and therefore we didn't have to include anything from her husband. If your surrogate is married then I would assume that point 7 above would also need to be done by the husband as well.

Whilst we were in the US we made sure that anything that would need to be signed by the surrogate was signed and notarised. And on top of this, because we were in the US for a while, we were able to also make sure that any document was signed after the children were 6 weeks old.

This made sure that all of the documents complied with UK law and the birth mother's rights to keep the child for up to 6 weeks post birth. One thing to note is that the actual application can be made at any time after the birth of the child, but the documents from the surrogate must be dated after the 6 week period is up.

Obviously, if you have to fly back to the UK before that time, you can leave anything that the surrogate needs to sign with her and ask her to do it after the 6 weeks are up. The Senior High Court Judge will need to see the originals, therefore the surrogate should sign anything needed and post it so that you have the originals with you when you go to the High Court.

We ended up having two hearings in the High Court with the Judge. The first was to discuss the points in the Act and to perform a box ticking exercise to make sure that we actually complied with the law. The most important part of this meeting was for her to ask us about how much money we had paid our surrogate and why we believed that the amount of money we had given her could be deemed a 'reasonable expense' as per the law.

We went through the logic of why we wanted a family, why we chose to do it in the US and of course we were fully open about all of the costs involved. We explained to the Judge why we thought the money we paid was reasonable. The Judge took everything that we said on-board and made notes in a computer whilst we were talking. She then said that on behalf of the Family Court it was the Judge's belief that it was in the children's best interest for us to be granted the Parental Order and for her to retrospectively approve the payments made to the surrogate as reasonable.

The only sticking point was that the Parental Order Reporter had not actually filed the report that would give CAFCASS' opinion on whether they believed us having the children would be in their best interest. This was a pure formality, as we knew that it wasn't a problem, but the Judge had to then put in process a formal request for the report to be filed– a process that the reporter was given 6 weeks to do.

When that was finally done, we appeared once again in the court for our second hearing where, within 15 minutes, we were granted all of the rights and responsibilities of parents in the eyes of the UK. A VERY joyous day for us all!

So that you have an idea of how long the application process can potentially take, for us it took from November 8th 2012, when we handed in the application, until July 22nd 2013, when we received the court order; just under 8 months!

Up to this point we had not applied for the children's UK passports. Although Steven has a visa to live and work in the UK, he doesn't actually have a UK passport and therefore his child is not entitled to a UK passport. As I'm British, mine is. Therefore, with the court order granting me full rights to both children, they were now deemed to be both mine and therefore they are both entitled to a UK passport.

Two weeks after our second hearing with the Judge the actual court order came through in the post, and I then used that to fill out UK passport applications for our children using Steven as parent one and me as parent two. We also had to include the original US birth certificates, which I was worried about getting lost in the post. However, because we'd ordered so many extra copies when we were in the US it didn't really matter.

We also received a letter stating that we were able to apply for re-registration of the birth certificates as the children now had us as parents. I filled out the paperwork that they needed as well as sending the requisite fee. A couple of weeks later the last two pieces of bureaucracy finally appeared through the post. The first were their re-registered UK birth certificates, and then finally their UK passports.

Questions to ask at this point

a) Do you want to use a UK law firm to do the Parental Order process for you?

b) Do you comply with all of the points in Section 54 to apply for a Parental Order?

c) Have you got all of the documentation ready and signed where necessary for the Parental Order?

d) Will you be able to submit the paperwork within 6 months of the child's birth?

e) Have you met the CAFCASS appointed Parental Order Reporter?

f) Has the Reporter submitted their report to CAFCASS?

g) Have you got two copies of everything so you can send one copy in with the C51 application and give one copy to the Judge on the day (in case the first copy gets lost)?

27 Costs

So there you have it. That is our story from start to finish with almost all of the ups and downs of having children via surrogacy in the US. It does seem like a massive amount of information to take on-board, and I would suggest that you read each chapter over and over. Obviously every surrogacy story will be different, but the general procedure remains the same. Hopefully this book will enable you to ask specific questions of anyone that you are talking to about going through surrogacy.

However, there is one major point that I haven't really spoken about in any great detail. That is how much this whole thing cost us. I have not intentionally left the amount of money that this process cost to the end of the book – I bet you couldn't wait anyways and skipped to this bit first (I know I would have done) - but it just seems that there was nowhere else logical for me to put it without putting you off the whole surrogacy process!

There is no question about it – surrogacy, and especially doing it in the US, is a very expensive thing to do. One of the predominant reasons that I am writing this book is because I believe that with increased transparency there should hopefully be a reduction in the costs as more and more intended parents understand the process and can manage a way to reduce their costs.

As intended parents you need to manage this process from a financial standpoint incredibly carefully as you do not want to get half way through the process only to run out of money. You will have to transfer a lot of the money up front into the escrow account, but that does not account for things like new-born health insurance, immigration or the Parental Responsibility Order process – all very key parts to the puzzle.

As much as we can try to get the professionals involved to reduce their costs, this will always be a business for many people and, of course, most businesses exist to make money! Steven and I really don't like the fact that there are people in the world who are unable to have a family because they can't afford it, and therefore we will do everything we can to get the costs down and the number of parents via surrogacy up!

So, down to actual numbers – in a nutshell we ended up spending a lot more money than anyone said we would, and we are still not sure if this was our fault or theirs – although it was more than likely ours!

As I've mentioned before we were originally quoted that the total for the surrogacy journey should cost us between $110,000 and $125,000. In fact our total was around $191,000, which is a big difference!

Admittedly, along the way we took the most expensive options as we thought that would guarantee us the best outcomes. Now that I have been through it I actually do not think that this is necessarily the case. We did end up with exactly what we wanted though, and the day your children are born you just forget the costs – it is, after all, a complete sunk cost (the money has been spent and whatever you do you won't get it back) and to see our dream come true really is priceless.

The rough breakdown on where the money we spent was:

- Surrogacy agency and extra expenses – $55,000
- IVF clinic – $53,000
- Surrogate (total including all expenses for travel, C-section and a twins fee) – $35,000
- Insurance premium and co-pay – $34,000
- Egg donor – $8,000
- Legal fees in Arizona – $6,000

Then, on top of this, one has to include the three flights that we took to the US, hotel accommodation, car hire and all of the other things that went along with us being in the US for over 2 months. This adds up as well.

Two things that I haven't included in this total are the cost of our maternity nurse and the cost of the nurse to look after Angela for the week after her surgery, as the reality is that those are nothing to do with the total cost of the surrogacy process.

So as you can see we spent a lot of money on creating our family. I am positive that if we were to go through it now knowing what we do then it would not cost us as much money as it did.

28 Final Thoughts

We are regularly asked whether or not we are going to have any more children, and I think that the answer depends on numerous factors, the most important of which is the cost. If money were no object, then I would have all of our frozen embryos transferred over the next few years and have a huge family. The reality is that we will have to wait and see.

I'm also asked what would I do differently. Another tricky question. Now that I know the process from start to finish I really think that we could make it a lot more streamlined and a lot cheaper.

Firstly we would not be relying on other people for information that we need to make the decisions that we need to make. Secondly we would be able to make the whole process more efficient and therefore more cost effective. However, assuming we kept everything the same as we did the first time round, the two main things that I would do differently are:

- I would keep a diary of what, when and why we did what we did – a lot of this book has been written along the way when we were making our decisions, but it doesn't actually still convey the full emotions behind what we were doing. I think that having a diary detailing every thought and emotion that we had at specific times would be something really lovely for our children to be able to look at in the years to come.
- I would choose an East Coast surrogate – as much as we love Angela, travelling to Arizona was physically further and also time-zone wise was difficult. There are multiple daily flights to the East Coast so, no matter what, we would be able to get there quickly and not have huge jet-lag.

If you can stretch financially to the cost of surrogacy in the US, then do not let the total cost of the process put you off having a family. The US is the most expensive option globally but the legal framework and Steven and I are doing everything that we can to make this whole process more open and transparent which hopefully will mean that the total cost should eventually start to come down.

We both really hope that you have found this book a useful source of information and if you want to contact us to talk about any points in it then please go to www.guidetosurrogacy.com and use the 'contact-us' form and we will get back to you as soon as possible.

One final thing to bear in mind as my mother says, "Where there is a will, there is a way" so don't give up – the end result is so incredibly worth every penny spent.

Appendix 1 – Parental Responsibility Orders

(1) On an application made by two people ('the applicants'), the court may make an order providing for a child to be treated in law as the child of the applicants if—

(a) the child has been carried by a woman who is not one of the applicants, as a result of the placing in her of an embryo or sperm and eggs or her artificial insemination,

(b) the gametes of at least one of the applicants were used to bring about the creation of the embryo, and

(c) the conditions in subsections (2) to (8) are satisfied.

(2) The applicants must be—

(a) husband and wife,

(b) civil partners of each other, or

(c) two persons who are living as partners in an enduring family relationship and are not within prohibited degrees of relationship in relation to each other.

(3) Except in a case falling within subsection (11), the applicants must apply for the order during the period of 6 months beginning with the day on which the child is born.

(4) At the time of the application and the making of the order—

(a) the child's home must be with the applicants, and

(b) either or both of the applicants must be domiciled in the United Kingdom or in the Channel Islands or the Isle of Man.

(5) At the time of the making of the order both the applicants must have attained the age of 18.

(6) The court must be satisfied that both—

(a) the woman who carried the child, and

(b) any other person who is a parent of the child but is not one of the applicants (including any man who is the father by virtue of section 35 or 36 or any woman who is a parent by virtue of section 42 or 43), have freely, and with full understanding of what is involved, agreed unconditionally to the making of the order.

(7) Subsection (6) does not require the agreement of a person who cannot be found or is incapable of giving agreement; and the agreement of the woman who carried the child is ineffective for the purpose of that subsection if given by her less than six weeks after the child's birth.

(8) The court must be satisfied that no money or other benefit (other than for expenses reasonably incurred) has been given or received by either of the applicants for or in consideration of—

(a) the making of the order,

(b) any agreement required by subsection (6),

(c) the handing over of the child to the applicants, or

(d) the making of arrangements with a view to the making of the order,

unless authorised by the court.

(9) For the purposes of an application under this section—

(a) in relation to England and Wales, section 92(7) to (10) of, and Part 1 of Schedule 11 to, the Children Act 1989 (c. 41) (jurisdiction of courts) apply for the purposes of this section to determine the meaning of 'the court' as they apply for the purposes of that Act and proceedings on the application are to be 'family proceedings' for the purposes of that Act, (b)in relation to Scotland, 'the court' means the Court of Session or the sheriff court of the sheriffdom within which the child is, and

(c)in relation to Northern Ireland, 'the court' means the High Court or any county court within whose division the child is.

(10)Subsection (1)(a) applies whether the woman was in the United Kingdom or elsewhere at the time of the placing in her of the embryo or the sperm and eggs or her artificial insemination.

(11)An application which—

(a)relates to a child born before the coming into force of this section, and

(b)is made by two persons who, throughout the period applicable under subsection (2) of section 30 of the 1990 Act, were not eligible to apply for an order under that section in relation to the child as husband and wife,

may be made within the period of six months beginning with the day on which this section comes into force.

Appendix 2 – List Of Things To Buy

With kind permission from our maternity nurse Desiree, here is the list of things that we bought when the children were first born.

Health and Hygiene/Bathing

- Diapers (nappies)
- Wipes
- Diaper rash cream
- Baby bath towels
- Baby washcloths
- Bath soap/shampoo (pump dispenser)
- Baby lotion (pump dispenser)
- Infant nail-clippers (one)
- Pacifiers (dummies)
- Nasal aspirator (the one from the hospital is the best)
- Vaseline (a squeeze tube, if having a boy and he is being circumsized)
- Infant thermometer

Feeding

- Bottles and all correct parts for the bottles you will be purchasing (if you are getting a make only available in the US, make sure that you get ALL nipples sizes so that when you are back in the UK you are not hunting for them online)
- Formula
- Burp cloths (20 or so)

Laundry

- Baby detergent (wash all clothes before babies are born)
- Stain remover

Clothing and Bedding

- A going home outfit
- Socks (preemie size)
- New-born gowns or sleepers (6–8)
- Onesies (short sleeve, no legs, 10 or so. Please buy long sleeve ones as well if baby is born in fall or winter)
- Sleepers (long sleeve, long legs, 10 or so)
- Swaddling blankets

Nursery Furniture/Gadgets

- Crib of some sort for the baby to sleep in
- Sound machine to provide white noise

On the Go

- Car seat (make sure you buy one that has a base that can be used in both the US and the UK as well as for the next size up – an expensive mistake to make otherwise – as we know!)
- Diaper bag
- Stroller (pram)
- Travel size baby wipes
- Hand sanitizer

Appendix 3 – The Routine For The Twins

This is the routine that the twins had from the day they were born until about 6 months old when it changed slightly.

07:00	Wake baby, change and feed. After feeding, play and keep baby awake until about 8:00 / 8:30
08:00 / 08:30	Watch for sleepy signs and, when you see them, lay baby down
10:00	Wake baby, if not already awake, change and feed. After feed, play and keep baby away until about 11:30
11:30	Watch for sleepy signs and, when you see them, lay baby down
13:00	Wake baby up, if not already awake, change and feed.
14:30	Watch for sleepy signs and, when you see them, lay baby down
16:00	Wake baby up, if not already awake, change and feed. Watch for sleepy signs and, when you see them, lay baby down for a little catnap. Let baby sleep for no more than 20 minutes. After you wake the baby up, they are going to be a bit crabby. That is to be expected, as you interrupted their nap.
18:00	Start night-time routine.
18:30	Feed baby.
19:00	Lay baby down for bed.

I don't think that we got too caught up in making sure that the times on this schedule were 100% accurate every day but it is more to see the routine of it. We feel that our children know what they are supposed to be doing at every stage of their day and that helps them a lot. Please note, that when your baby reaches around 6 months old, the routine changes slightly to a 4-hourly routine instead of a 3-hourly routine.

07:00	Feed
09:00 - 11:00	Nap #1
11:00	Feed
12:30	Solids, if applicable
13:00-15:00/15:30	Nap #2
15:00	Feed
18:00	Night-time routine
19:00	Bed

Appendix 4 - Travel Consent Form Filled Out By The Surrogate

<u>AFFIDAVIT OF '*SURROGATE*'</u>

I, *full name of surrogate* declare as follows:

1. I am the birth mother of, *full name of child 1* & *full name of child 2* ('Children') born on

2. *Full name of father 1* and *Full name of father 2* ('Fathers') are the biological parents of *child 1* and *child 2* respectively.

3. I have full knowledge of, and hereby consent to, each of the Fathers travelling with the Children without my presence, wherever they may choose with either one traveling with both Children.

4. Specifically, I consent to the Fathers travelling to the United Kingdom and anywhere in the United States with the Children.

5. I also have full knowledge of, and hereby consent to, either one of the fathers traveling alone with both children.

6. If there are any questions, please call me at *surrogate's telephone number.*

Signed under the pains and penalties of perjury this ___ day of month, year.

_____

Signed by *full name of surrogate*

STATE OF *XXX*

On this _____ day of *month, year* before me, the undersigned notary public, personally appeared name of surrogate, proved to me through satisfactory evidence of identification, to be the person who signed the preceding or attached document in my presence, and who swore or affirmed to me that the contents of the document are truthful and accurate to the best of her knowledge and belief.

Date: _____

State of *XXX*

County of _____

_____

_____

Notary Public

My Commission Expires:

5934802R00077

Printed in Great Britain
by Amazon.co.uk, Ltd.,
Marston Gate.